ICONS AND IDOLS

SPORTS | NOV. 3, 2017 | LOS ANGELES, CA

PUBLIC EXHIBITION & LIVE AUCTION LOCATION

JULIEN'S AUCTIONS
805 North La Cienega Blvd. | Los Angeles, CA
Monday, October 30 - Saturday, November 4, 2017
10:00 a.m. Pacific Time – 5:00 p.m. Pacific Time Daily
Free to the public.

EXHIBITION & LIVE AUCTION LOCATION

JULIEN'S AUCTIONS
805 North La Cienega Blvd. | Los Angeles, CA

LIVE AND ONLINE AUCTION

FRIDAY, NOVEMBER 3, 2017
Icons and Idols: Sports
Session I: 10:00 a.m. Pacific Time, Lots 1– 165

SATURDAY, NOVEMBER 4, 2017
Icons & Idols: Rock "n" Roll
Session II: 10:00 a.m. Pacific Time, Lots 166– 439
Session III: 2:00 p.m. Pacific Time, Lots 440– 689

cover photo: HANS DERYK/AP/REX/Shutterstock

For inquiries, please contact Julien's Auctions:
phone: (310) 836-1818 | fax: (310) 742-0155
email: info@juliensauctions.com

Julien's Auctions Mailing Address:
8630 Hayden Place | Culver City, CA 90232

Julien's *Live*

Julien's Auctions will broadcast live streaming video of the auction and provide viewers with real-time, interactive bidding during the auction. Online viewers can watch the auction in real-time and bid live against the bidders in the room, phone bidders, proxy bidders and other collectors from around the world. You may also place bids online in the weeks leading up to the auction.

Visit www.juliensauctions.com

Sale Number 3190

email: info@juliensauctions.com
www.juliensauctions.com
www.juliensauctions.co.uk

DARREN JULIEN President / CEO, darren@juliensauctions.com

MARTIN J. NOLAN Executive Director, martin@juliensauctions.com

NAN VALENTINO Chief Operating Officer, nan@juliensauctions.com

JASON DEBORD Social Media Manager, social@juliensauctions.com

GABY DOUEK Gallery Manager, gaby@juliensauctions.com

MICHAEL EDWARDS Assistant Shipping Manager, mike@juliensauctions.com

SUMMER EVANS Director of Photography, summer@juliensauctions.com

NATE HEBRON Director of Warehouse Operations and Shipping, nate@juliensauctions.com

MITCHELL KABA Property Specialist, mitch@juliensauctions.com

NANCY KAPITANOFF Content Editor, nkapitanoff@juliensauctions.com

DANIEL KRUSE Auctioneer

RICARDO LIMON Warehouse Manager, ricky@juliensauctions.com

JENNIFER LORENZI Costume & Fashion Specialist, jennifer@juliensauctions.com

TIM LUKE Auctioneer - Executive Director, Street and Contemporary Art, tim@juliensauctions.com

NIMA MAHDJOUR Data Manager, nima@juliensauctions.com

MEGAN MAHN MILLER Senior Property Specialist, megan@juliensauctions.com

REBECCA MARKMAN Antiques & Fine Art Specialist, rebecca@juliensauctions.com

DARCIE MENA Accounting, darcie@juliensauctions.com

ADRIANA RAMOS Property Receiver, adriana@juliensauctions.com

MICHAEL D. RIES Catalogue Design

HILLARY ANNE RIPPS Executive Offices, hillary@juliensauctions.com

ALFONSO ROMERO Assistant Warehouse Manager, alfonso@juliensauctions.com

VINCENT SANDOVAL Freelance Photographer

JACLYN SOBEL Client Services, jaclyn@juliensauctions.com

JASON WATKINS Assistant Shipping Manager, jason@juliensauctions.com

DREW WOOD IT Specialist

LAURA WOOLLEY Consultant, Sales Specialist

ISABEL YEO Property Manager and Specialist, isabel@juliensauctions.com

EXERCICESPHYSIQUES ET SPORTS

1
RUBENS BARRICHELLO
2011 F1 RACE WORN WILLIAMS FIRESUIT
A Sparco brand firesuit race worn by former Williams driver and 11-time Formula 1 Grand Prix winner Rubens Barrichello during the 2011 Formula 1 season. On the front waist is a Brazilian flag representing Barrichello's home country next to lettering that reads "Ruben." The front features AT&T, PDVSA, and Oris logos, along with secondary sponsor logos on the shoulders and sleeves. On the inside zipper seam is embroidered lettering that reads "RB-003-11-D," along with a stitched-on Sparco tag. The back of the suit has the AT&T/Williams and Randstad logos. The back collar features an embroidered FIA Sport (Fédération Internationale de l'Automobile) logo and reads "Standard 8856-2000/ RS.192.10/ Sparco/ Year of manufacture: 2011."

$1,500-3,000

2
2005 MARK WEBBER WILLIAMS F1 PRACTICE WORN FIRESUIT
A 2005 Puma brand Formula 1 firesuit worn by Mark Webber during practice for the Williams F1 team during the 2005 season. Stitched onto the front left at hip level are the Australian flag and an embroidered "M. Webber." To the right is the Puma logo. The suit features the RBS logo on the front upper left and the Bridgestone logo on the front upper right. On the right sleeve are the logos for Allianz, Petrobras, and RBS. On the left sleeve are logos for Allianz, Bud, and RBS. On each shoulder is the FedEx logo. Around the collar is the Puma logo. On the back of the suit is the Puma logo. The back collar features an FIA (Fédération Internationale de l'Automobile) logo and reads "Standard 8856-2000/ RS.075/04/ Puma/ Year of manufacture: 2005."

$800-1,000

3
RALF SCHUMACHER WILLIAMS F1 TESTING WORN FIRESUIT
A Formula 1 firesuit worn by Ralf Schumacher while testing for Williams F1 racing. Stitched onto the front of the suit at waist level are "Ralf Schumacher" in embroidered lettering and the German flag. The suit features the BMW logo on the front upper right and the BMW Williams F1 team logo on the upper back. Schumacher drove for Williams from 1999 to 2004. BMW sponsored Williams F1 racing from 2000 to 2005.

$800-1,200

4
AYRTON SENNA 1986 F1 RACE USED REAR TIRE
A 1986 Goodyear Eagle Formula 1 rear tire with Speedline rim, raced used by Ayrton Senna during the 1986 F1 season when he drove for Lotus in the Lotus 98T. On the tire is the identification "26.0 x 15.0 - 13/ Radial/ For Racing Purposes Only." Both the tire and the rim are marked "12," Senna's number, in handwritten pink numbering.

Diameter, 25 1/4 inches

$1,000-2,000

5
SEBASTIAN VETTEL RED BULL RACING F1 RACE USED WHEEL

A Sebastian Vettel race used OZ Racing brand front left wheel from a Red Bull Racing Formula 1 race car. The magnesium alloy wheel features an inset ring design that bisects the 10 spokes leading to the wheel hub. The wheel has a number decal that shows the letters "FL," along with a German flag emblem signifying Vettel's home country. Former Red Bull team driver Vettel is among the most successful F1 drivers of all time, being one of only four to have won four or more F1 World Drivers' Championships.

14 3/16 by 14 3/16 by 12 5/8 inches

$1,000-1,200

6
SEBASTIAN VETTEL RED BULL RACING F1 RACE USED WHEEL

A Sebastian Vettel race used OZ Racing brand front right wheel from a Red Bull Racing Formula 1 race car. The magnesium alloy wheel features an inset ring design that bisects the 10 spokes. The wheel has a number decal that shows Vettel's racing number 1, which he used from 2011 to 2014, the letters "FR," and a German flag emblem signifying Vettel's home country. At the 2013 Indian Grand Prix, at the Buddh International Circuit in India, Vettel sealed the Drivers' Championship title and in doing so won the Constructors' Championship for Infiniti Red Bull Racing for the fourth consecutive year.

14 3/16 by 14 3/16 by 12 5/8 inches

$1,200-2,000

7
SEBASTIAN VETTEL 2010s RED BULL RACING F1 RACE USED WHEELS
A race used group of four OZ Racing brand front wheels from a Red Bull Racing Formula 1 race car. The magnesium alloy wheels feature an inset ring design that bisects the 10 spokes. Two of the wheels have a decal that shows Sebastian Vettel's racing number 1, which he used from 2011 to 2014, letters showing the wheel's position on the car, and a German flag emblem signifying Vettel's home country. Being one of only four drivers to have won four or more Drivers' titles, Vettel is among the most successful F1 drivers of all time.

$4,000-6,000

8
NICO ROSBERG WILLIAMS F1 RACE WORN BOOTS
A pair of Sparco brand boots race worn by Nico Rosberg during 2006-2009, when he drove for the Williams Formula 1 team. Written on the interior of each boot tongue are Rosberg's initials "NR" in black marker. Attached to the inside of each tongue is Sparco's "Made in Italy" tag. The German-born Rosberg retired from racing after posting 23 Formula 1 victories and winning the 2016 Formula 1 World Drivers' Championship.

$600-800

9
NICO ROSBERG 2006 WILLIAMS F1 CHINESE GRAND PRIX SAMPLE BOOTS
A pair of Puma brand Williams Formula 1 boots worn by German driver Nico Rosberg for fitting for the 2006 Chinese Grand Prix. The 16th race of the season, it was held on October 1, 2006, at Shanghai International Circuit. The Puma inventory tag on the right boot is dated September 5, 2006, and states the pair is a "Fit & Wear Test Sample" for Rosberg for the Williams F1 season and that the boots are size 42.

$600-800

10
NICO ROSBERG WILLIAMS F1 RACE WORN GLOVES
A pair of Sparco brand gloves race worn by German driver Nico Rosberg when he drove for the Williams Formula 1 team from 2006 to 2009. On the inside of each glove are Rosberg's initials "NR" in black marker. The gloves feature the logo of longtime Williams sponsor Oris Swiss watches. A Sparco tag affixed to the palm side of the right glove states the gloves are "In compliance with FIA Standard 8856-2000."

$600-800

11
SACHIN TENDULKAR FAREWELL TO A CRICKET LEGEND
SIGNED LIMITED EDITION CRICKET BALL DISPLAY
A Sachin Tendulkar Farewell To A Cricket Legend limited edition cricket ball set, number 224/300, featuring the signature of Tendulkar on the white ball in black marker. A celebration of Tendulkar's career, the set includes two balls that display his record-breaking achievements, a brief biography with an authenticity hologram from A-Tag affixed to it, and a certificate of authenticity from A-Tag. The balls are housed in a wood display case. Among his lifetime of achievements in cricket, Tendulkar played more Tests than any other cricketer and achieved the first double-century in a One Day International, the most Test centuries in history, and the most One Day International centuries in history. Born in Mumbai, India, he made his Test debut in 1989 against Pakistan at age 16 and would represent Mumbai domestically and India internationally for almost 24 years.

Case, 11 by 4 7/8 by 3 7/8 inches

$1,000-2,000

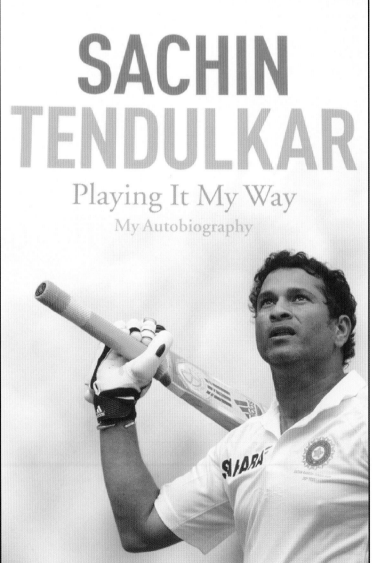

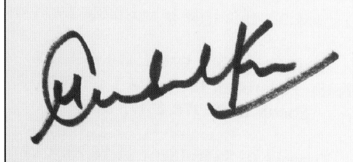

12
SACHIN TENDULKAR
SIGNED FIRST EDITION AUTOBIOGRAPHY
A first edition copy of Sachin Tendulkar's autobiography, *Sachin Tendulkar: Playing It My Way* (London: Hodder & Stoughton, 2014), signed by Tendulkar on the title page in black marker.

9 1/2 by 6 3/8 inches

$1,000-2,000

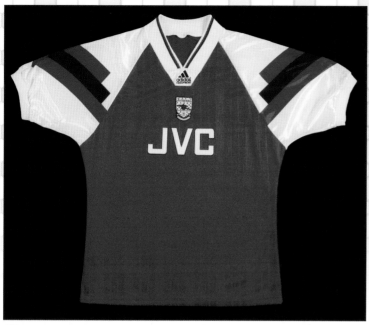

17
JOHN JENSEN 1992 ARSENAL MATCH WORN JERSEY
An Adidas brand Arsenal FC jersey worn by Danish footballer John Jensen during the 1992 preseason. Jensen was part of the 1992-1993 Arsenal team that won the FA Cup and the 1993-1994 team that won the European Cup Winners' Cup. On the Danish national team during the 1992 UEFA European Football Championship, he scored the opening goal in Denmark's 2-0 victory over Germany in the final. Embroidered on the front center of the jersey is the Arsenal logo. Stitched on the back of the jersey is Jensen's uniform number 17.

$800-1,000

18
GEORGE BEST SIGNED MANCHESTER UNITED RETRO 1968 JERSEY
A Toffs brand Manchester United retro 1968 jersey signed and inscribed by legendary Northern Irish footballer George Best on his number 11 on the back of the jersey "Best Wishes George Best" in black marker. In 1968, Best won the European Cup with Manchester United and was named the European Footballer of the Year and the Football Writers' Association Footballer of the Year. The jersey is accompanied by a certificate of authenticity for the signature from Route One Memorabilia and a letter of authenticity for the signature from JSA. Size S.

$600-800

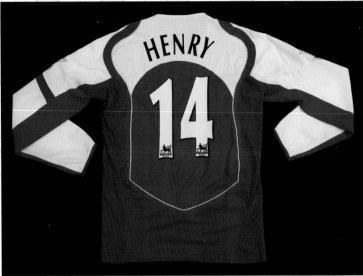

19
THIERRY HENRY 2004 ARSENAL FC MATCH WORN JERSEY
A Nike brand long-sleeve Arsenal FC jersey match worn by Thierry Henry in a match against Chelsea FC in the later half of 2004. Henry played for Arsenal from 1996-2007. He is the club's all-time record goalscorer. Each sleeve of the jersey features the 2003-2004 Champions Premier League patch. Arsenal ended the 2003-2004 season without a single defeat, the first team ever to do so in a 38-game league season. Size L.

$800-1,200

20
ROY KEANE 2002 MANCHESTER UNITED TEAM ISSUED JERSEY
A Nike brand Manchester United FC jersey team issued to Roy Keane during the 2002-2004 seasons. Keane played for Manchester United from 1993-2005 and became the club captain in 1997. He scored his 50th goal for the team on February 5, 2005. His appearance in the 2005 FA Cup final, which United lost to Arsenal, was his seventh appearance in an FA Cup final, a record at the time. He was inducted into the English Football Hall of Fame in 2004. Size XL.

$200-400

21
CESC FÀBREGAS SIGNED 2010 ARSENAL FC MATCH WORN JERSEY
A Nike brand 2010-2011 Arsenal FC home jersey match worn by Cesc Fàbregas and signed by him on his uniform number 4 on the back of the jersey in black marker. The 2010-2011 season was Fàbregas' last season with Arsenal. The jersey is accompanied by a letter of authenticity for the signature from JSA. Size L.

$400-600

22
PAUL SCHOLES TESTIMONIAL TEAM SIGNED JERSEYS AND PENNANT SET
A group of two commemorative football jerseys, one Manchester United and one New York Cosmos, and a commemorative pennant from the Paul Scholes Testimonial match organized by Manchester United to honor Scholes' career with the club. The match between Manchester United and New York Cosmos was played on August 5, 2011, at Old Trafford in Manchester, England. Manchester United won 6-0 with Scholes scoring the first goal. Scholes played his entire 17-year football career with Manchester United, winning 10 Premier League titles. The Nike brand Manchester United jersey features over 20 signatures of team players, all signed in black marker. The Umbro brand Cosmos jersey features 10 signatures by Cosmos team members in blue marker. The pennant was presented to Scholes by the Cosmos team. It features the embroidered Manchester United and Cosmos emblems and the embroidered text "Presented To/ Paul Scholes/ By The Board, Management & Team Of/ The New York Cosmos/ To Commemorate The Occasion Of His/ Testimonial/ And In Celebration Of/ His Outstanding Career/ (1994-2011)/ August 5/ 2011." The Manchester United jersey is accompanied by a letter of authenticity for the signatures from PSA/DNA.

$1,000-2,000

23
SENINHO 1980 NEW YORK COSMOS MATCH WORN JERSEY
An Ellesse brand 1980 New York Cosmos football team jersey match worn by Arsénio Rodrigues Jardim, known simply as Seninho, during a friendly match with the Greece national football team on July 1, 1981, at Giants Stadium in East Rutherford, New Jersey. Cosmos won the match 2-0. Seninho played for Cosmos from 1978-1982, winning three North American Soccer League titles with the team. Stitched onto the front of the jersey are the Cosmos logo patch and Seninho's number 11 in blue tackle twill numbering. His number 11 is also stitched on the right sleeve and the back of the jersey in blue tackle twill numbering. Also stitched on the back of the jersey is "Seninho" in blue tackle twill lettering.

$800-1,200

24
ALEX OXLADE-CHAMBERLAIN
MATCH WORN FOOTBALL BOOTS
A pair of Nike brand football boots worn by Arsenal FC player Alex Oxlade-Chamberlain during the 2015-2016 season. On the outer side of each boot is an image of the English flag and "Chambo."

$300-400

25
KIERAN GIBBS MATCH WORN FOOTBALL BOOTS
A pair of Adidas brand football boots match worn by Arsenal FC footballer Kieran Gibbs during the 2016-2017 season. On the outer side of the right boot is "Gibbo 3." On the back of the left boot is a handwritten 3, his uniform number.

$200-400

26
LAURENT KOSCIELNY MATCH WORN FOOTBALL BOOTS
A pair of Nike brand Tiempo boots match worn by Arsenal FC footballer Laurent Koscielny during the 2016-2017 season. On the outer side of the left boot are the names of his children, Maina and Noah. The children's names are also on the right boot, next to an image of the French flag, but the "h" is missing from Noah.

$300-400

27
PAOLO DI CANIO CELTIC MATCH WORN BOOTS
A pair of Pantofola d'Oro football boots match worn by Paolo Di Canio when he played for Celtic football club during the 1996-1997 season. During his playing career Di Canio made over 500 league appearances and scored over 100 goals.

$400-600

28
**JIMMY JOHNSTONE 1972 CELTIC BOBBY CHARLTON
TESTIMONIAL MATCH WORN JERSEY**
An Umbro brand long-sleeve Celtic home jersey match worn by
Jimmy Johnstone during the September 18, 1972, Bobby Charlton
Testimonial match between Celtic and Manchester United. The
teams played to a 0-0 draw in the match that honored the
legendary England and Manchester United footballer. Johnstone
was on the Celtic team that won the then European Cup in 1967. He
made 515 appearances for Celtic, scoring 129 goals. In 2002, he was
voted Celtic's best player ever by the club's fans. On the interior
collar of the jersey "J. Johnston [sic]" is written in blue ink. The
Umbro tag stitched into the interior collar has "J J" written on it in
blue ink. Size 38/40.

$2,000-4,000

29
**KENNY DALGLISH 1977 CELTIC
SCOTTISH CUP FINAL MATCH WORN JERSEY**
An Umbro brand Celtic jersey match worn by Kenny Dalglish
during the 1977 Scottish Cup Final between Celtic and
Rangers. Celtic won the match played on May 7 at Hampden
Park in Glasgow, Scotland, 1-0. Embroidered on the front
upper right of the jersey is "Scottish Cup Final 1976/77." The
jersey is accompanied by a letter detailing a history of the
jersey's ownership including its residence on the wall of the
bar beside Celtic Park. Size 38.

$3,000-4,000

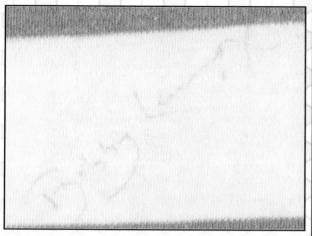

30
ROY AITKEN WORN BOBBY LENNOX SIGNED 1978 CELTIC SCOTTISH LEAGUE CUP FINAL JERSEY
An Umbro brand long-sleeve jersey match worn by Roy Aitken during the March 18, 1978, Scottish League Cup Final between Celtic and Rangers and signed by Bobby Lennox in blue ink. Rangers won the match 2-1 in extra time. Lennox, MBE (Member of the Order of the British Empire), was a member of Celtic's 1967 European Cup winning team known as the Lisbon Lions, which defeated Inter Milan 2-1 at the Estádio Nacional stadium in Lisbon, Portugal. He won 11 League medals, eight Scottish Cup medals, and five League Cup medals. In 2002, Celtic supporters voted him a member of the club's all-time greatest team. Aitken played for Celtic from 1976-1990, making 486 appearances for the team, the third most in club history. On the front upper left of the jersey is the Celtic club crest, which did not appear on the team's jerseys until the 1977-1978 season. The design is based on a 1930s Celtic club crest. The jersey is accompanied by a certificate of authenticity for the signature from JSA.

$1,500-3,000

31
DANNY McGRAIN 1982 CELTIC MATCH WORN EUROPEAN CUP JERSEY
An Umbro brand Celtic home jersey worn by Danny McGrain during the European Cup match between Celtic and Real Sociedad on November 3, 1982. Celtic defeated Real Sociedad, 2-1. McGrain played 659 competitive matches for Celtic between 1970 and 1987, winning seven League Championships, five Scottish Cups, and two Scottish League Cups. With 62 caps for the Scottish national team, he was inducted into the Scottish Football Hall of Fame in 2004. The jersey is accompanied by a letter stating the jersey was worn in this match from The Football Museum. Size M.

$1,500-3,000

32
OWEN ARCHDEACON 1985 CELTIC MATCH WORN JERSEY
An Umbro brand long-sleeve Celtic football club away jersey match worn by Owen Archdeacon during 1985. Archdeacon joined Celtic in 1984 and was a member of the 1985-1986 team that won the league on the last day of the season in a 5-0 win against St Mirren at Celtic Park.

$800-1,200

33
BRIAN McCLAIR
1985 CELTIC MATCH WORN JERSEY
An Umbro brand Celtic football club home jersey match worn by Brian McClair during the 1985-1986 season. McClair's goals helped Celtic to a league championship win in 1985-1986; two of the five goals in Celtic's 5-0 victory over St Mirren on the last day of the season came from McClair. In four seasons with Celtic, McClair made 204 appearances in all competitions and scored 126 goals. With the team, he won the 1985 Scottish Cup and the 1986 Scottish Premier Division.

$600-800

34
TONY SHEPHERD 1986 CELTIC DUBAI SUPER CUP MATCH WORN JERSEY
An Umbro brand Celtic football club jersey worn by Tony Shepherd during the 1986 Dubai Super Cup played on December 9 between Liverpool, the champions of England, and Celtic, the champions of Scotland, at the Al Wasl stadium in Dubai, United Arab Emirates. Liverpool won the match on penalties, 4-2. Size M.

$600-800

35
PETER GRANT 1986 CELTIC MATCH WORN JERSEY
An Umbro brand Celtic football club home jersey match worn by Peter Grant during the Celtic vs. St Mirren match on May 3, 1986, which Celtic won 5-0 to earn the league championship on the last day of the season.

$800-1,200

36
FRANK McAVENNIE DOUBLE-SIGNED 1988 CELTIC CENTENARY MATCH WORN JERSEY
An Umbro brand long-sleeve 1988 Celtic football team home jersey match worn by Frank McAvennie during the 100th anniversary season of the club and double-signed by him on the front and with an inscription on the back, "Be Lucky" in black marker. The embroidered Celtic emblem celebrates the 100th anniversary with the years "1888 1988." The jersey is accompanied by a letter of authenticity for the signatures from JSA. Size L.

$800-1,200

37
ANDY WALKER SIGNED 1989 CELTIC SCOTTISH CUP FINAL MATCH ISSUED JERSEY
An Umbro brand Celtic home jersey team issued to Andy Walker for the 1988-1989 Scottish Cup Final match between Celtic and Rangers, signed and inscribed "Good Luck and Best Wishes/ Andy Walker" in black marker on the front of the jersey. Walker played for Celtic from 1987-1991. The front upper left of the jersey features the Celtic logo and the embroidered text "S.F.A. Cup Final/ 1988/89." The jersey is accompanied by a letter of authenticity for the signature from JSA. Size L.

$1,000-1,500

38
PAUL McSTAY 1989 CELTIC MATCH WORN JERSEY
An Umbro brand long-sleeve Celtic football club away jersey match worn by Paul McStay during the 1989-1991 seasons. McStay, MBE (Member of the Order of the British Empire), spent his entire career with Celtic, from 1982-1997. He helped Celtic win three league titles, the last one in 1988.

$600-1,000

39
NORMAN WHITESIDE 1983 NORTHERN IRELAND NATIONAL TEAM MATCH WORN JERSEY
An Adidas brand long-sleeve Northern Ireland national football team jersey match worn by Norman Whiteside during the 1983-1985 seasons. Whiteside holds records as the youngest player in a World Cup and the youngest player to score in a League Cup and an FA Cup final. He won 38 caps for Northern Ireland, played in the 1982 and 1986 World Cups, and helped Northern Ireland win the last British Home Championship in 1984. Playing for Manchester United from 1982-1989, he scored 68 goals in 278 league and cup appearances for the club. Embroidered on the front upper left of the jersey is the logo of the Irish Football Association, the organization that governs the Northern Ireland national football team. Affixed to the back of the jersey is Whiteside's uniform number 10 in white numbering. Size M.

$800-1,200

40
FRANK STAPLETON 1981 REPUBLIC OF IRELAND MATCH WORN JERSEY
An O'Neills brand Republic of Ireland national football team home jersey match worn by Frank Stapleton during the September 9, 1981, World Cup Qualifier between Ireland and the Netherlands. The teams played to a 2-2 draw, with Stapleton scoring one of Ireland's goals. Stapleton earned 71 caps for the Republic of Ireland, scoring a then record 20 goals. He began his football career with Arsenal, followed by Manchester United, and played for the Republic of Ireland team from 1976-1990. Stitched on the back of the jersey is Stapleton's number 10 in white cloth numbering. Size 41-42.

$1,000-2,000

41
1966 WORLD CUP ENGLAND JULY 30, 1966, FINAL MATCH TICKET
An original ticket from the 1966 FIFA World Cup final match, which took place on July 30, 1966, at Wembley Stadium (originally known as Empire Stadium) in Wembley Park, London, England. England defeated West Germany 4-2 in the final match to win its only World Cup to date. The back of the ticket features the ticket number, 1678.

$200-300

ASOCIACION URUGUAYA DE FOOTBALL

(FORMULARIO PARA LLENAR Y DEVOLVER A LA SECRETARIA)

Division Campeonato Mundial Serie

Club Brasil contra Club Jugoslavia

Jugado en Parque Central el dia 14 Julio de 1930

Empezado a las 15 terminado a las 17

Club Brasil Club Jugoslavia

(ESCRIBASE LOS NOMBRES CON CLARIDAD)

N.o Carnet	NOMBRES Y APELLIDOS	N.o Carnet	NOMBRES Y APELLIDOS
1	Joel de Oliveira Monteiro	1	M. Jakšitch
2	Alfredo Brilhante da Costa	2	M. Ivkovitch
3	Luiz Gervazoni	3	D. Mihajlovitch
4	Hermogenes Fonseca	4	Arsenijevitch
5	Fausto dos Santos	5	Stefanovitch
6	Fernando Giudicelli	6	Djokitch
7	Polycarpo Ribeiro	7	Tirnanitch
8	Nilo Murtinho Braga	8	Marjanovitch
9	Araken Patusca	9	Beck
10	João Coelho Netto	10	Vujadinovitch
11	Theophilo Bittencourt Pereira	11	Sekulitch

EL JUEZ DEBE EXIGIR LA PRESENTACION DE LOS CARNETS

Firmado João Coelho Netto Capitan Firmado Militin Ivkovitch Capitan

Goals hechos por 1

Resultado uno goal Resultado dos goal

Juez [signature]

Domicilio

JUECES DE TOQUE

DOMICILIOS

Goals hechos por 2

ASOCIACION URUGUAYA DE FOOTBALL

(FORMULARIO PARA LLENAR Y DEVOLVER A LA SECRETARIA)

Division Campeonato Mundial Serie

Club Uruguay contra Club Peru

Jugado en Estadio Centenario el dia 18 de Julio de 1930

Empezado a las 3,15 terminado a las 5

Club Uruguay Club Peru

(ESCRIBASE LOS NOMBRES CON CLARIDAD)

N.o Carnet	NOMBRES Y APELLIDOS	N.o Carnet	NOMBRES Y APELLIDOS
1	Enrique Ballestero	1	Pardon
2	José Nasazzi	2	Mario de las Casas
3	Domingo Tejera	3	Maquilon
4	José L. Andrade	4	Denegri
5	Lorenzo Fernandez	5	Galindo
6	Alvaro Gestido	6	Astengo
7	Santos Urdinaran	7	Lavalle
8	Hector Castro	8	Flores
9	Pedro Petrone	9	Villanueva
10	José P. Cea	10	Neyra
11	Santos Iriarte	11	Souza

EL JUEZ DEBE EXIGIR LA PRESENTACION DE LOS CARNETS

Firmado Nasazzi Capitan Firmado Antonio Maquilon Capitan

Goals hechos por Castro 1

Resultado uno goal Resultado cero goal

Juez John Langenus

Domicilio Hotel Las Palmas

JUECES DE TOQUE

H. Christophe Balway

DOMICILIOS

Belge France

Goals hechos por

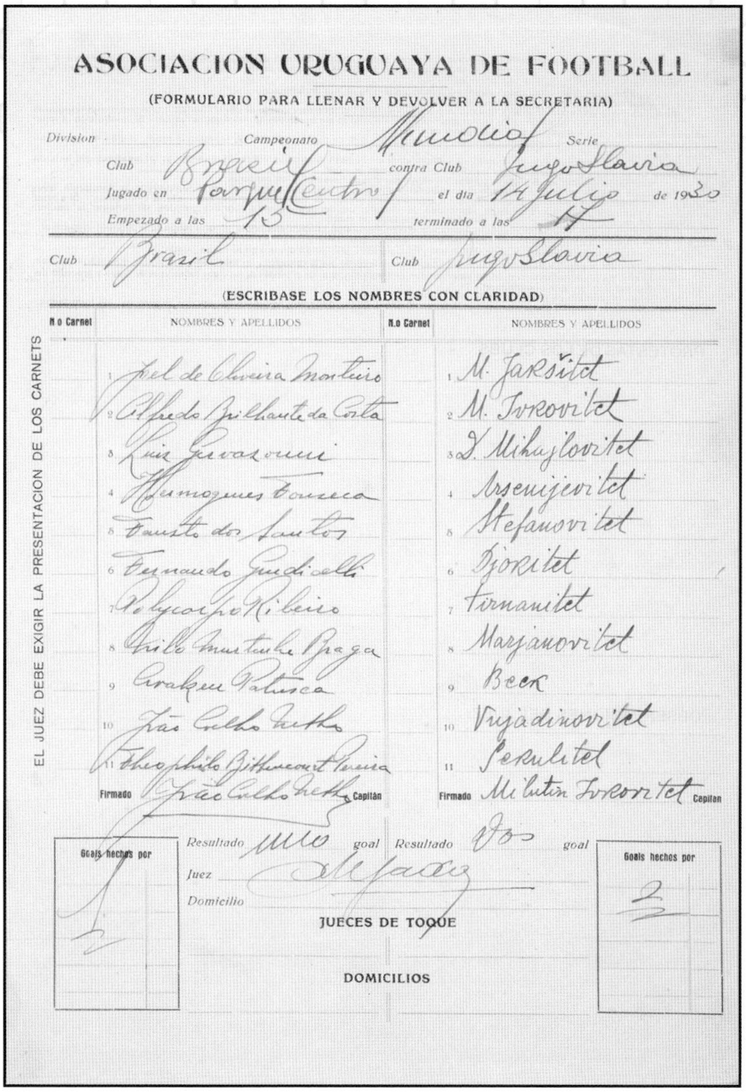

42
1930 FIFA WORLD CUP
BRAZIL VS. YUGOSLAVIA MATCH DOCUMENT

An original document from the 1930 FIFA World Cup match that took place on July 14, 1930, between Brazil and Yugoslavia at Montevideo, Uruguay's Parque Central. The document features the lineups for the teams, the results of the match with Yugoslavia defeating Brazil 2-1, and the signature of the judge. The 1930 World Cup was the inaugural World Cup. Uruguay defeated Argentina in the final, 4-2.

13 1/4 by 8 3/4 inches

$800-1,000

43
1930 FIFA WORLD CUP
URUGUAY VS. PERU MATCH DOCUMENT

An original document from the 1930 FIFA World Cup match that took place on July 18, 1930, between Uruguay and Peru at Montevideo, Uruguay's Estadio Centenario. The document features the lineups for the teams, the results of the match with Uruguay defeating Peru 1-0 when "Castro" scored the goal, and the signatures of the judges. The 1930 World Cup was the inaugural World Cup. Uruguay defeated Argentina in the final, 4-2.

13 1/4 by 8 3/4 inches

$800-1,000

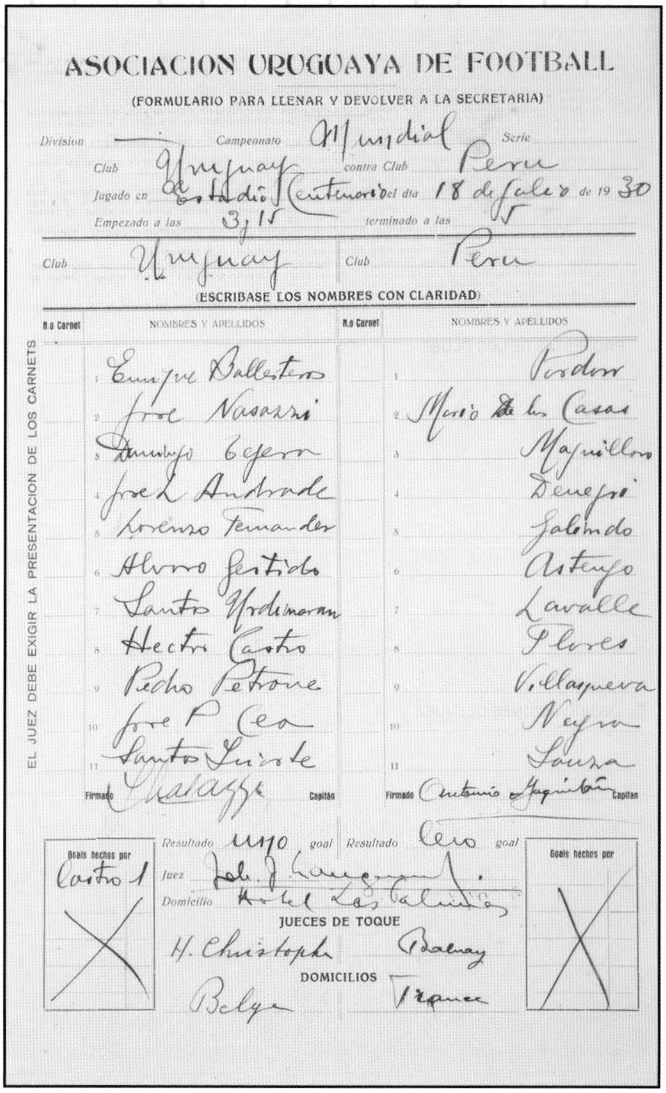

44
MARIO KEMPES 1978 ARGENTINA WORLD CUP TROPHY
A 1978 World Cup trophy presented to Argentina national football team goalkeeper Mario Kempes by the Republic of Argentina Secretary of Sport for his performance in Argentina's 1978 World Cup victory. Kempes was the leading goalscorer in the tournament, scoring six goals. Two were against the Netherlands in the final, which Argentina won 3-1. His second was the game winner in extra time. He received the Golden Boot as top goalscorer and the Golden Ball as the player of the tournament. The trophy features a stylized version of the FIFA World Cup trophy. The trophy stands on a wood base with a metal plaque with the text "Republica Argentina/ Secretaria de Deporte/ A/ Mario Kempes/ Goleador."

6 1/2 by 2 1/4 by 2 1/4 inches

$2,000-4,000

45
MICHEL PLATINI 1994 FIFA WORLD CUP PASS
A 1994 FIFA World Cup pass issued to Michel Platini. Considered one of the all-time greatest football players, Platini won the Ballon d'Or three times, in 1983, 1984, and 1985, and was sixth in the FIFA Player of the Century vote. He was named Chevalier of the Legion of Honour in 1985 and became Officier in 1988. The 1994 FIFA World Cup took place in nine cities across the United States from June 17 to July 17, 1994. Brazil defeated Italy in the final match 3-2 in a penalty shootout after the match ended 0-0 in extra time, the first World Cup final to be decided on penalties.

$400-600

46
RONALDINHO 2006 FIFA WORLD CUP BRAZIL MATCH WORN JERSEY
A Nike brand Brazil national football team jersey worn by Ronaldinho during the 2006 FIFA World Cup in Germany in the June 22 match between Brazil and Japan. The front upper left of the jersey features the Brazilian Football Confederation (CBF) logo with five stars, symbolizing Brazil's five World Cups in 1958, 1962, 1970, 1994, and 2002. At the center is Ronaldinho's number 10. On the right sleeve is the FIFA World Cup Germany 2006 logo patch. On the back of the jersey are "Brasil" in yellow lettering and "Ronaldinho" and his number 10 in green lettering and numbering. The jersey is accompanied by a letter from a previous owner who states he was given the jersey by Brazil national team kit man Rogelson Barreto. Size L.

$1,000-2,000

47
KAKÁ 2010 FIFA WORLD CUP QUALIFIERS BRAZIL MATCH WORN JERSEY
A Nike brand jersey worn during a 2010 World Cup Qualifiers match by Brazil national football team member Ricardo Izecson dos Santos Leite, known simply as Kaká, and signed by all players capped for the match in which Kaká wore this jersey. The yellow jersey features a Nike logo, CBF emblem, and number 10 on the front. On the right sleeve is a 2010 FIFA World Cup Qualifiers patch. On the back of the jersey is "Brasil" lettering at the back of the collar above a number 10. The jersey is signed on the front in black marker by 23 players from the Brazil national football team including Doni, Júlio César, Dani Alves, Lúcio, Maicon, Thiago Silva, Elano, Felipe Melo, Gilberto Silva, Josué, Júlio Baptista, Kaká, Michel Bastos, Grafite, Luís Fabiano, Nilmar, Lucas Leiva, and Hulk.

$800-1,200

48
CRISTIANO RONALDO 2010 PORTUGAL NATIONAL TEAM WORLD CUP MATCH ISSUED JERSEY
A Nike brand Portugal national football team jersey issued to Cristiano Ronaldo for the 2010 World Cup match between Portugal and Brazil on June 25, 2010, in Durban, South Africa. The teams played to a 0-0 draw. The front upper left of the jersey features an embroidered Portugal national football team emblem. Below the emblem is the text "Portugal/Brasil/ 25/6/2010." Affixed to the right sleeve is the FIFA World Cup South Africa 2010 logo patch. Size L.

$400-600

49
ALEXIS SÁNCHEZ CHILE NATIONAL TEAM 2014 WORLD CUP QUALIFIERS MATCH WORN JERSEY
A Puma brand Chile national football team jersey match worn by Alexis Sánchez in the October 16, 2012, World Cup Qualifiers match between Chile and Argentina at the Estadio Nacional in Santiago, Chile. Argentina won the match 2-1. Affixed to the right sleeve is the 2014 FIFA World Cup Brazil Qualifiers patch. Affixed to the left sleeve is the FIFA My Game Is Fair Play patch. Size S.

$800-1,200

50
2014 FIFA WORLD CUP BRAZIL VS. GERMANY SEMI-FINAL MATCH USED FOOTBALL

An Adidas brand Brazuca official match ball used in the 2014 FIFA World Cup semi-final match between Brazil and Germany on July 8, 2014, in Belo Horizonte, Brazil's Estadio Mineirão. Germany defeated Brazil, 7-1, the largest margin of victory in a FIFA World Cup semi-final. While this ball was used in the match as described, FIFA officials neglected to affix a "Match Used" sticker to the ball after the match. Size 5.

$2,000-4,000

51
DAVID LUIZ BRAZIL 2014 WORLD CUP MATCH WORN AND TEAM SIGNED JERSEY

A Nike brand Brazil national football team jersey match worn by David Luiz during the 2014 World Cup in Brazil and signed by 13 members of the team: Jefferson, Dani Alves, Marcelo, Hulk, Júlio César, Dante, Henrique, Ramires, Hernanes, Willian, Bernard, Jô, and Victor. The front upper left of the jersey features the Brazilian Football Confederation (CBF) logo with five stars symbolizing Brazil's five World Cups in 1958, 1962, 1970, 1994, and 2002. At the center is Luiz's number 4. On the right sleeve is the 2014 FIFA World Cup Brasil logo patch. On the left sleeve is the FIFA Football For Hope logo patch. On the back of the jersey are "David Luiz" and his number 4 in green lettering and numbering. Size XL.

$1,000-2,000

52
2014 WORLD CUP BRAZIL TROPHY
A 2014 FIFA World Cup trophy gifted to high-ranking FIFA officials after the opening match of the 2014 FIFA World Cup in Brazil. On June 12, 2014, in Sao Paulo, Brazil defeated Croatia 3-1 in the first match. Neymar scored twice. Brazil last hosted the World Cup in 1950. The trophy features the image of an athletic figure with arms outstretched in victory and the words "FIFA / WORLD CUP." A plaque on the base of the trophy reads "FIFA World Cup/ Brasil" with the 2014 World Cup logo and "Opening match, 12th June 2014, Sao Paulo/ Brazil vs Croatia."

$1,500-2,000

53
1950 WORLD CUP BRAZIL JULES RIMET TROPHY
A 1950 FIFA World Cup Jules Rimet Trophy awarded to Aníbal Paz, the goalkeeper of the World Cup winning Uruguay national football team. The 1950 FIFA World Cup took place in Rio de Janeiro, Brazil, from June 24 to July 16, 1950. Host nation Brazil and Uruguay met in the final match, with Uruguay winning the final in a shocking defeat of Brazil, 2-1. According to Guinness World Records, "Officially, 173,850 paid spectators crammed into Rio de Janeiro's Maracanã Stadium on July 16, 1950, to watch host Brazil take on Uruguay. ... Some estimates have even pegged the attendance as high as 199,000 or 210,000 unofficially." The Brazilian spectators were shocked by Brazil's loss and immediately went into mourning. Brazil had been so heavily favored to win that a set of winner's medals engraved with the Brazilian players' names before the game ended could not be presented. Jules Rimet himself presented the FIFA World Cup trophy to the Uruguayan team on the field, without a formal ceremony or speech, while grieving Brazilian players looked on and spectators headed to the exits. Paz was a Uruguayan and South American top goalkeeper. From 1939 to 1953, he played for Club Nacional de Football, winning the Uruguayan championship nine times. This golden tone Jules Rimet Trophy was designed by S.A.B.U. Broncherais Uruguay. It stands on a black wood base.

Length, 11 1/2 inches; Weight, 3.4 pounds

$4,000-6,000

54
1998 FIFA WORLD CUP GOLD MEDAL

A 1998 FIFA World Cup France gold medal gifted to high-ranking FIFA officials after the World Cup. The medal is the same version that is presented to the players with the exception of the top loop and ribbon. The tournament took place in 10 cities in France from June 10 to July 12, 1998. France won the tournament, defeating Brazil 3-0 in the final. The medal features the text "Coupe Du Monde/ De La FIFA/ France 1998" and the name of the manufacturer, G.D.E. Bertoni of Italy, on one side. On the other side is a relief image of the World Cup trophy with an athletic figure with arms outstretched in victory and the text "FIFA/ World Cup." The medal is housed in a FIFA frame case.

Case, 4 1/4 by 4 1/8 by 1 3/8 inches

$4,000-6,000

55
1998 WORLD CUP BRAZIL VS. FRANCE COMMEMORATIVE LIMITED EDITION PENNANT

A limited edition pennant celebrating France's victory in the 1998 FIFA World Cup. The pennant features an embroidered 1998 FIFA World Cup France official logo, embroidered images of the Brazilian and French flags, and embroidered text commemorating France's 3-0 victory score in the final match that took place on July 12, 1998, at the Stade de France in Saint-Denis, France.

18 by 14 5/8 inches

$200-400

56
2002 FIFA WORLD CUP PARTICIPANT FINAL COMPETITION MEDAL

A gold tone Participant Final Competition medal presented during the 2002 FIFA World Cup that took place in South Korea and Japan. One side of the medal features a relief image of the World Cup trophy with an athletic figure with arms outstretched in victory and the text "FIFA/ World Cup." On the other side are the text "Participant Final Competition/ 2002/ FIFA World Cup/ Korea Japan" and the name of the manufacturer, G.D.E. Bertoni of Italy. The medal is housed in a FIFA frame case.

Case, 4 1/4 by 4 by 1 3/8 inches

$1,000-1,500

57
2006 FIFA WORLD CUP GERMANY GOLD MEDAL

A FIFA World Cup Germany 2006 gold medal gifted to high-ranking FIFA officials after the World Cup. The tournament took place from June 9 to July 9, 2006, in Germany. In the final match, Italy defeated France 5-3 in a penalty shootout after extra time ended in a 1-1 draw. The medal is the same version that is presented to the players from the winning team, with the exception of the top loop and ribbon. It features a relief image of the World Cup Germany 2006 logo on one side with the text "FIFA World Cup/ Germany/ 2006" and the name of the manufacturer, G.D.E. Bertoni of Italy. On the other side is a relief image of the World Cup trophy with an athletic figure with arms outstretched in victory and the text "FIFA/ World Cup." The medal is housed in a FIFA frame case.

Case, 4 1/8 by 4 by 1 3/8 inches

$3,500-4,500

58
2009 FIFA WORLD PLAYER GALA MEDAL

A 2009 FIFA World Player Gala medal, gifted to the players and high-ranking FIFA officials after the Player of the Year award ceremony that took place on December 21, 2009, in Zürich, Switzerland. Lionel Messi was the FIFA World Player of the Year, and Marta, who then played for the United States' Los Angeles Sol, the Brazil national team, and Santos FC, was the FIFA Women's World Player of the Year. The medal features the FIFA logo on one side and on the other the text "FIFA® World Player Gala 2009/ Zurich 21 December 2009" surrounded by the raised lettering "Federation Internationale/ De Football Association." The medal is housed in its original case that features the FIFA logo inside.

Case, 7 1/8 by 6 1/4 by 1 1/2 inches; Medal diameter, 2 11/16 inches

$2,000-3,000

59
1994 FIFA WORLD CUP GOLD WINNER'S MEDAL

A 1994 FIFA World Cup gold winner's medal awarded to a player from the champion Brazil national football team. The 1994 FIFA World Cup took place in nine cities across the United States from June 17 to July 17, 1994. Brazil defeated Italy 3-2 in a penalty shootout after the game ended 0-0 in extra time, the first World Cup final to be decided on penalties. Brazil became the first nation to win four World Cup titles. The team won a fifth title in 2002. One side of the medal features a relief image of the World Cup trophy with an athletic figure with arms outstretched in victory and the words "FIFA/ World Cup." On the other side is "FIFA/ World Cup/ USA/ 1994." The medal hangs from a red, white, and blue ribbon, the colors of the American flag. It is housed in a black case.

Medal diameter, 2 inches; Case, 7 5/8 by 7 9/16 by 1 5/8 inches

$45,000-55,000

60
2004 FIFA 100 YEARS MEDAL
A gold tone medal marking the May 20, 2004, Brazil vs. France match at the Stade de France in Saint-Denis, France, played to commemorate FIFA's 100th anniversary, from 1904 to 2004. The teams played to a 0-0 draw. The medal features the FIFA logo with the text "100 Years/ 1904-2004" below "Federation Internationale De Football Association" (FIFA). On the other side, surrounding the medal is the raised lettering "Federation Internationale/ De Football Association." The medal is housed in its original FIFA case.

Medal diameter, 2 11/16 inches; Case, 4 by 3 7/8 by 1 1/8 inches

$800-1,200

61
PELÉ 2004 FIFA CENTENNIAL ORDER OF MERIT MEDAL AND CERTIFICATE
An Order of Merit medal and certificate presented to Pelé in 2004 by the Fédération Internationale de Football Association (FIFA), from Pelé's personal collection. In 2004, FIFA honored two of football's greatest players, Pelé and Franz Beckenbauer. The paper certificate features the FIFA centennial emblem, addresses Pelé's and Beckenbauer's various accomplishments, and states that "Since ending his playing career, Pelé has performed many valuable services for our game, both as Minister of Sport and a world-renowned ambassador for football." The gold tone medal features the FIFA globe emblem with lettering that reads "FIFA Centennial/ Fédération Internationale de Football Association/ 100 Years/ 1904 - 2004/ Order of Merit." A blue and gold ribbon is affixed to the clasp at the top of the medal. The certificate is housed in its original FIFA case.

Case length, 12 3/4 inches; Medal diameter, 1 3/4 inches

$3,000-5,000

62
PELÉ 1954 INSCRIBED AMÉRICA FC 50TH ANNIVERSARY MEDAL

A medal owned by Pelé commemorating the 50th anniversary of the América Football Club (AFC) located in Rio de Janeiro, Brazil. The club was founded on September 18, 1904. The medal features the AFC team logo along with the words "Cinqüentenário De Fundação" (Fiftieth Anniversary of Foundation). The other side features a low relief image of a woman holding a laurel wreath over the AFC home stadium called the Estádio Giulite Coutinho, with Rio's Corcovado mountain and Christ the Redeemer statue in the background. The rim is inscribed "Ao fabuloso PELÉ uma lembrança da Torcida Americana 19-11-61."

Diameter, 2 inches

$600-800

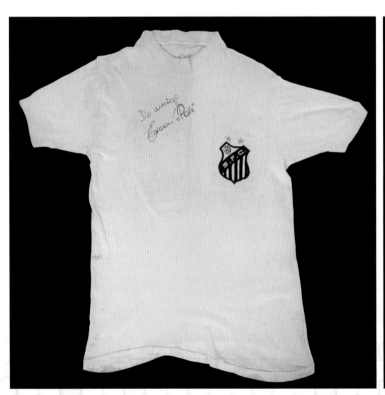

63
PELÉ SIGNED 1969 SANTOS FC MATCH WORN JERSEY

A Santos FC jersey match worn by Pelé in 1969 and signed by him with the inscription "Do amigo/ Edson + Pelé" at a later date in black marker.

$2,500-4,000

64
PELÉ *ESCAPE TO VICTORY* CAST SIGNED JERSEY

A Toffs brand cotton long-sleeve football jersey signed by Pelé and eight other cast members of the film *Escape To Victory* (titled *Victory* in North America) (Lorimar, 1981), all of them professional football players. Signatures include Ossie (Osvaldo) Ardiles, Kevin Beattie, Kevin O'Callaghan, Russell Osman, Laurie Sivell, Mike Summerbee, Robin Turner, and John Wark. In the film, Pelé starred alongside Sylvester Stallone and Michael Caine as Nazi prisoners conscripted to play a propaganda football match during World War II that they would then use as a diversion for their escape. The jersey is accompanied by a letter of authenticity for the signatures from PSA/DNA. Size M.

$800–1,200

65
PELÉ SIGNED CANVAS IMAGES PAIR

A pair of large canvases, one of them a color image of the Brazilian and Italian national football teams in advance of the final match of the 1970 FIFA World Cup on June 21, 1970, in Mexico City's Estadio Azteca. Brazil would defeat Italy 4-1 to win its then third World Cup. The image is signed by Pelé in black marker. The other canvas features a black and white image of Pelé embracing Muhammad Ali and kissing him on the cheek at Pelé's final professional football game as a member of the New York Cosmos. The game took place at Giants Stadium in East Rutherford, New Jersey, on October 1, 1977. Pelé presented Ali with a game ball used in the match. The canvas is signed by Pelé "Edson = Pelé" in black marker. Each canvas is accompanied by a certificate of authenticity for the signature from PSA/DNA.

World Cup canvas, 28 by 20 1/8 inches; Ali-Pelé canvas, 29 by 24 inches

$1,000–2,000

66
1970 WORLD CUP FINAL GOALSCORERS SIGNED BRAZIL JERSEY

An Athleta brand replica of the 1970 Brazil national football team jersey that the team wore when it won its third World Cup, signed in black marker by Pelé and his teammates Gerson, Jairzinho, and Carlos Alberto, who scored the four goals to win the final match. Stitched on the front upper left of the jersey is the Confederação Brasileira de Desportos (CBD, Brazilian Sports Confederation) emblem, as the Brazilian Football Confederation was known in 1970. Stitched on the back of the jersey is Pelé's number 10 in green tackle twill numbering. The signatures are accompanied by a certificate of authenticity from PSA/DNA.

$600-800

67
PELÉ SIGNED 1958, 1962, AND 1970 WORLD CUP BRAZIL JERSEYS GROUP

A group of three jerseys signed by Pelé, each jersey a replica of the Brazil national football team jersey worn in one of the first three World Cups Brazil won. The blue 1958 Brazil World Cup jersey and the 1962 long-sleeve World Cup jersey are signed "Pelé" in black marker. The 1970 Brazil World Cup jersey is signed and inscribed "Pelé/ 3 X WC. Champ" in black marker. Below Pelé's signature is the text "Brazil 4-1 Italy/ Mexico 1970 World Cup final/ June 21 1970." Each jersey is accompanied by a certificate of authenticity for the signature from PSA/DNA.

$1,000-2,000

68
PELÉ AND MUHAMMAD ALI SIGNED CANVAS FROM LAST GAME

A large black and white image on canvas of Pelé embracing Muhammad Ali and kissing him on the cheek at Pelé's final professional football game as a member of the New York Cosmos. The game took place at Giants Stadium in East Rutherford, New Jersey, on October 1, 1977. Pelé presented Ali with a game ball used in the match. The canvas is signed by both Pelé and Ali in gold marker. Affixed to the bottom corner are Muhammad Ali and Pelé authenticity holograms for the signatures.

40 1/2 by 30 by 1 1/4 inches

$8,000-12,000

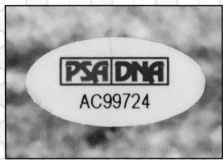

PSA DNA
AC99724

Certificate of Authenticity

This item has been examined by one or more PSA/DNA experts and it is our opinion that the item is genuine. The item has been permanently marked with a proprietary invisible ink, containing a patented strand of synthetic DNA.

Certification Number: AC99715

Verification inquiries can be made to PSA/DNA by calling 800-325-1121 or by visiting psacard.com and entering the certification number above.

Joe Orlando
President, PSA/DNA

Examined and Certified

69
PELÉ SIGNED "BICYCLE KICK" PHOTOGRAPHS GROUP
A group of 10 prints of black and white photographs featuring Pelé's famous bicycle kick. The image was originally captured in a game against Belgium in 1968. Each photograph is signed "Pelé" and in black marker. Nine of the photographs are accompanied by individual certificates of authenticity from PSA/DNA. Affixed to the 10th photograph is PSA/DNA authentication sticker number AC97627; however, no certificate is present for that photograph.

Each, 16 by 20 inches

$1,500-2,000

70
PELÉ SIGNED BRAZIL NATIONAL FOOTBALL TEAM JERSEY
A Brazil national football team replica jersey signed by Pelé in silver marker on his iconic uniform number 10 on the back of the jersey. Size XL. The jersey is accompanied by a letter of authenticity for the signature from JSA.

$400-600

71
ROBERTO CARLOS 2003 BRAZIL MATCH WORN JERSEY
A Nike brand Brazil national football team jersey match worn by Roberto Carlos. The yellow jersey features the Brazilian Football Confederation (CBF) embroidered crest applied to the top left, with five embroidered stars above representing Brazil's five World Cup victories. Applied to the center front of the jersey is Carlos' jersey number 6 in green numbering, with the jersey number repeating on the back. Stitched into the collar of the jersey is a Nike manufacturer tag displaying the size as "L."

$400-600

72
CAFU 2004 BRAZIL MATCH WORN JERSEY
A Nike Brazil national football team long-sleeve jersey match worn by Marcos Evangelista de Morais, known simply as Cafu. The yellow jersey features the Brazilian Football Confederation (CBF) crest applied to the top center, with five stars above representing Brazil's five World Cup victories. Applied to the center front of the jersey is Cafu's jersey number 2 in green numbering within a circle, with the jersey number repeating on the back. Cafu is the most internationally capped male Brazilian player of all time. He represented Brazil in four FIFA World Cups between 1994 and 2006 and is the only player to have appeared in three consecutive World Cup finals. Brazil won the 1994 and 2002 World Cups. Size L.

$400-600

73
NEYMAR 2012 BRAZIL NATIONAL TEAM MATCH WORN JERSEY

A Nike brand 2012 Brazil national football team jersey match worn by Neymar. The front upper left of the jersey features the Brazilian Football Confederation (CBF) emblem with five stars representing Brazil's five World Cup victories in 1958, 1962, 1970, 1994, and 2002. At the center is Neymar's number 11. On the back of the jersey is Neymar's number 11 in yellow numbering.

$1,000-2,000

74
ANDRÉ SCHÜRRLE 2011 GERMANY NATIONAL FOOTBALL TEAM MATCH WORN JERSEY

An Adidas brand Germany national football team jersey match worn by André Schürrle during Germany's International Friendly match vs. Brazil that took place on August 10, 2011, at Mercedes-Benz Arena, in Stuttgart, Germany. Germany won the match 3-2. The front upper left of the jersey features the Germany national team emblem with three stars representing Germany's three World Cup championships in 1954, 1974, and 1990. On the upper right is Schürrle's number 9. On the back of the jersey are the script "Deutscher Fussball-Bund" (German Football Association) in gold lettering and "Schürrle" and his number 9 in black lettering and numbering. Size L.

$300-600

75
ZINEDINE ZIDANE 2001 FRANCE NATIONAL TEAM MATCH WORN JERSEY

An Adidas brand France national football team jersey match worn by Zinedine Zidane during the first half of a friendly match between France and Algeria on October 6, 2001, at the Stade de France in Saint-Denis, Paris. It was the first football match between these national teams since Algeria gained independence from France in 1962. France was leading 4-1 when at the 74th minute fans ran onto the pitch and the match was abruptly ended. Zidane presented this jersey on the field to Algerian player Omar Belbey. The front upper left of the jersey features the France national football team logo with the text "France/ Algerie/ 06-10-2001." Size L.

$5,000-7,000

76
RONALDINHO 2013 COPA LIBERTADORES ATLÉTICO MATCH WORN JERSEY

A Lupo Sport brand Clube Atlético Mineiro jersey match worn by Ronaldinho in the Copa Bridgestone Libertadores, South America's premier international club football tournament. Atlético Mineiro won the cup, defeating the Paraguayan club Olimpia on penalties in the final. The front upper left of the jersey features the Clube Atlético Mineiro logo. At the center are Ronaldinho's number 10 and the Banco BMG main sponsor logo. On the top right is the Lupo Sport logo. On the right sleeve is the Copa Bridgestone Libertadores logo patch. On the back of the jersey are the Lupo Sport and BMG logos and in black lettering and numbering Ronaldinho's number 10 and "Ronaldinho."

$600-800

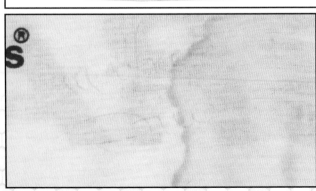

77
JÚNIOR FLAMENGO MATCH WORN JERSEY SIGNED BY ZICO

An Adidas brand Clube de Regatas do Flamengo football club, known simply as Flamengo, jersey match worn by Leovegildo Lins da Gama Júnior, known simply as Júnior, and signed by Zico with the inscription "Com abraço" (with a hug) in blue ink. Zico played for the Brazilian national football team from 1976-1986, scoring 48 goals in 71 appearances. On the front upper left of the jersey is the Flamengo logo. On the back of the jersey is Júnior's number 5 in black felt numbering. The jersey is accompanied by a letter of authenticity for the signature from JSA. Size G.

$600-800

78
LÚCIO 2006 FC BAYERN MUNICH MATCH WORN JERSEY
An Adidas brand FC Bayern Munich jersey match worn during the 2006-2007 season by Lucimar Ferreira da Silva, known simply as Lúcio. The jersey features the Adidas, FC Bayern Munich, and T-Com emblems on the front. On the right sleeve is the Bundesliga Deutscher Meister 2005/2006 emblem. On the left sleeve is the T-Com emblem. On the back of the jersey is "Bayern München" above his uniform number 3 and "Lucio." With Lúcio defending, Bayern Munich won the 2005-2006 Bundesliga title. Size XL.

$200-400

79
MICHAEL LAUDRUP 1997 AJAX MATCH WORN JERSEY
An Umbro brand long-sleeve Ajax jersey match worn by Danish football player Michael Laudrup during the 1997-1998 season, when he finished his playing career and Ajax won its league title. During his football career, Laudrup also won league titles with Barcelona, Real Madrid, and Juventus. Embroidered on the front center of the jersey is the Ajax emblem. Applied to the back of the jersey are "Laudrup" and his number 11 in white-on-red lettering and numbering. Size XL.

$400-600

80
PAUL McSTAY 1991 CELTIC SCOTTISH LEAGUE CUP FINAL MATCH WORN JERSEY
An Umbro brand long-sleeve Celtic home jersey match worn by Paul McStay in the 1990-1991 Scottish League Cup Final match between Celtic and Rangers. Rangers defeated Celtic 2-1 at Hampden Park. McStay, MBE (Member of the Order of the British Empire), spent his entire career with Celtic, from 1982-1997. He helped Celtic win three league titles, the last one in 1988. The front upper left of the jersey features the Celtic logo and the embroidered text "League Cup Final/ 1990/91." Written on the interior collar is "McStay" in blue ink. The jersey is accompanied by a letter of authenticity from The Celtic Shirt.

$800-1,200

81
PETER GRANT 1995 CELTIC MATCH WORN JERSEY
An Umbro brand long-sleeve 1995 Celtic football club home jersey worn by Peter Grant during the first half of the Scottish Cup Final match between Celtic and Airdrie. Celtic won the match, 1-0. Grant was the Man of the Match. The front upper left of the jersey features the Celtic football club emblem and below it the embroidered text "S.F.A. Cup Final/ 1995." Size XL.

$800-1,200

82
LUBO MORAVCÍK DOUBLE-SIGNED 2001 CELTIC UEFA MATCH WORN JERSEY
An Umbro brand Celtic football club away jersey match worn by Lubo Moravcík in the 2001 UEFA Cup match between Celtic and Valencia on November 22, 2001, that Valencia won, 1-0. Moravcík signed the jersey on the front and the back in black marker. The jersey is accompanied by a letter of authenticity for the signatures from JSA and a photograph of Moravcík holding the jersey. Size M.

$600-800

83
CHRIS SUTTON SIGNED 2001 CELTIC MATCH WORN JERSEY
An Umbro brand long-sleeve Celtic football team away jersey match worn by Chris Sutton in the August 25, 2001, match between Celtic and Hibernian, when he scored two goals in Celtic's 4-1 victory. Sutton signed the back of the jersey twice in black marker. The jersey is accompanied by a letter of authenticity for the signatures from JSA. Size XXL.

$400-600

84
JOOS VALGAEREN 2002 CELTIC UEFA CUP MATCH WORN JERSEY
An Umbro brand Celtic football club jersey match worn by Joos Valgaeren during the March 20, 2003, UEFA quarter-final match between Liverpool and Celtic at Anfield, in Liverpool, England. Celtic won the match 2-0, advancing to the UEFA semi-final, and to the UEFA final against Porto. Porto won the final match 3-2 in extra time. Size XXL.

$400-600

85
HENRIK LARSSON 2002 CELTIC MATCH WORN JERSEY
An Umbro brand Celtic football club home jersey match worn by Henrik Larsson during the 2002-2003 season, when Celtic reached the 2003 UEFA Cup final, its first final since 1970, courtesy of Larsson's goals in the semi-final matches. In 2003 Larsson was voted the Greatest Swedish Footballer of the Last 50 Years as part of the UEFA Jubilee Awards. He won four league titles in seven years with Celtic, scoring 242 goals in 315 competitive Celtic matches. Size L.

$400-600

86
JOHN HARTSON SIGNED 2003 CELTIC MATCH WORN JERSEY
An Umbro brand Celtic football club jersey match worn by John Hartson during the 2003-2004 season and signed by Hartson and inscribed "10" on the back of his jersey in his uniform number 10. The jersey is accompanied by a letter of authenticity for the signature from JSA. Size XL.

$300-400

87
CRAIG BELLAMY SIGNED 2005 CELTIC MATCH WORN JERSEY
An Umbro brand Celtic football club home jersey match worn by Craig Bellamy during the last three matches for the Scottish Premier League title. Celtic was defeated by Rangers in the final match. Bellamy signed the back of the jersey below his uniform number 47 in black marker. The jersey is accompanied by a certificate of authenticity for the signature from JSA.

$400-600

88
THOMAS GRAVESEN SIGNED 2006 CELTIC MATCH WORN JERSEY
A Nike brand Celtic football club home jersey match worn by Thomas Gravesen during the September 23, 2006, match between Celtic and Rangers, when he scored his first goal for Celtic. Celtic won the match 2-0. Gravesen signed the back of the jersey with the inscription "16" above his uniform number 16 in black marker. The jersey is accompanied by a letter of authenticity for the signature from JSA. Size L.

$400-600

89
KENNY MILLER SIGNED 2006 CELTIC TEAM ISSUED JERSEY
A Nike brand long-sleeve Celtic football club home jersey team issued to Kenny Miller for the September 23, 2006, match between Celtic and Rangers, when he scored his debut goal for Celtic. Celtic won the match 2-0. Miller signed the back of the jersey next to his uniform number 9 in black marker. The jersey is accompanied by a letter of authenticity for the signature from JSA. Size XL.

$200-400

90
LEE NAYLOR SIGNED 2006 CELTIC MATCH WORN JERSEY
A Nike brand long-sleeve 2006 Celtic football club home jersey match worn by Lee Naylor during the UEFA Champions League group match between Celtic and Manchester United at Celtic Park on November 21, 2006, in Glasgow, Scotland. Celtic won the match 1-0. Naylor signed the back of the jersey in black marker. The jersey is accompanied by a certificate of authenticity for the signature from JSA. Size M.

$300-400

91
MARC-ANTOINE FORTUNÉ SIGNED 2009 CELTIC MATCH WORN JERSEY
A Nike brand long-sleeve Celtic football team away jersey match worn by Marc-Antoine Fortuné during the November 22, 2009, match between Celtic and Dundee United. Fortuné signed the back of the jersey by his uniform number 10 in black marker. The jersey is accompanied by a letter of authenticity for the signature from JSA. Size L.

$300-500

92

FRASER FORSTER SIGNED 2014 CELTIC NATIONAL FAMINE MEMORIAL DAY TEAM ISSUED JERSEY

A Nike brand long-sleeve Celtic football club jersey team issued to goalkeeper Fraser Forster and signed by him and inscribed "Best Wishes" on the front and back of the jersey in silver marker. The jersey, issued for the May 11, 2014, match between Celtic and Dundee United, features an embroidered National Famine Memorial Day patch, a remembrance of the Great Famine, a period of mass starvation, disease, and emigration in Ireland between 1845 and 1852. On the front upper left of the jersey is the Celtic emblem that marks the club's then 125-year history, 1888-2013. In February 2014, Forster broke Bobby Clark's Scottish League record of 1,155 minutes without conceding a goal in a league match. The jersey is accompanied by a letter of authenticity for the signatures from JSA. Size L.

$600-1,000

93

NIR BITTON 2015 CELTIC NATIONAL FAMINE MEMORIAL DAY MATCH WORN JERSEY

A New Balance brand Celtic football team jersey match worn by Nir Bitton in the 2015 National Famine Memorial Day match between Celtic and Hearts on Saturday, September 26, at Celtic Park in Glasgow, Scotland. The teams played to a 0-0 draw. The jersey features an embroidered National Famine Memorial Day patch, a remembrance of the Great Famine, a period of mass starvation, disease, and emigration in Ireland between 1845 and 1852. Size M.

$400-600

94

VIRGIL VAN DIJK SIGNED 2015 CELTIC MATCH WORN JERSEY

A Nike brand Celtic home jersey worn by Virgil van Dijk during the Scottish League Cup Final on March 15, 2015, and signed by him in black marker on the back of the jersey under his uniform number 5. Celtic defeated Dundee United in the match, 2-0, for the team's 15th League Cup title. Celtic won the Scottish Premiership and was named the Professional Footballers' Association Scotland Team of the Year in both of van Dijk's seasons with the team. On the front center of the jersey is the text "The Scottish League Cup Final/ Presented by QTS/ 15th March 2015." On each sleeve is the Scottish League Cup patch. The jersey is accompanied by a letter of authenticity for the signature from JSA. Size L.

$600-800

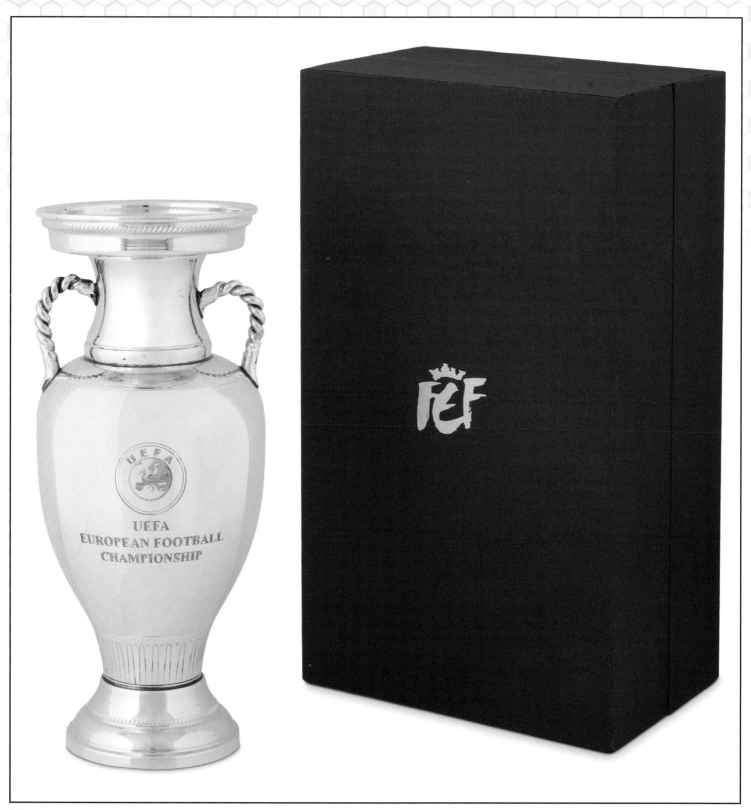

95
2008 UEFA EURO TROPHY

A 2008 UEFA Euro trophy awarded to the players of the Spain national football team by RFEF (Real Federación Española de Fútbol or Royal Spanish Football Federation). The 2008 UEFA Euro final match took place on June 29, 2008, at the Ernst-Happel-Stadion in Vienna, Austria. Spain defeated Germany 1-0. This was only the second time in European Championship history that the champions had won every match in the group stage; the other team to do so was France in 1984. This UEFA trophy is made of silver by Alegre Joyeros. The trophy features the UEFA logo with the words "FIFA/ European Football Championship." On the reverse is "Coupe Henri Delaunay" and all the national team winners since 1960. The trophy is housed in its original blue case.

Length, 7 7/8 inches

$2,500-3,500

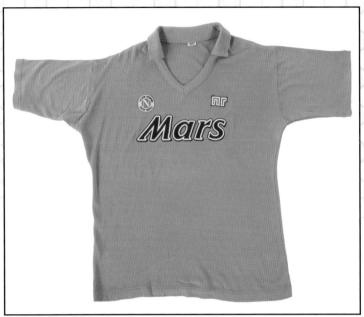

96
DIEGO MARADONA 1989 NAPOLI MATCH WORN JERSEY
An Ennerre (nr) brand Società Sportiva Calcio Napoli, known simply as Napoli, football team jersey match worn by legendary Argentine football player Diego Maradona during the 1989-1990 season. On the front upper right of the jersey is the Napoli logo. On the upper left is the Ennerre brand logo. The center of the jersey features the Mars main sponsor logo. Stitched on the back of the jersey is Maradona's uniform number 10 in white numbering. Napoli won its second league title in 1989-1990, the UEFA Cup in 1989, and the Italian Super Cup in 1990.

$1,500-3,000

97
DIEGO MARADONA 1989 NAPOLI TEAM ISSUED JERSEY
An Ennerre (nr) brand Società Sportiva Calcio Napoli, known simply as Napoli, football team third jersey match worn by legendary Argentine football player Diego Maradona during the 1989-1990 season. The crest of the Italian flag is stitched into the front upper left of the jersey. The center of the jersey features the Mars main sponsor logo. Stitched into the left arm of the jersey is a Società Sportiva Calcio Napoli patch. Applied to the back of the jersey is Maradona's uniform number 10 in white numbering. Napoli won its second league title in 1989-1990, the UEFA Cup in 1989, and the Italian Super Cup in 1990.

$800-1,200

98
MICHEL PLATINI 1984 JUVENTUS MATCH WORN JERSEY
A Kappa brand long-sleeve Juventus Football Club jersey match worn by Michel Platini during the 1984-1985 season. The front upper left of the jersey features Juventus' emblem. On the back of the jersey is Platini's uniform number 10. Platini won the Serie A title with Juventus in 1984 and 1986, the European Cup Winners' Cup in 1984, the European Super Cup in 1984, the European Cup in 1985, and the Intercontinental Cup in 1985. He finished as top scorer in Serie A in 1982-1983, 1983-1984, and 1984-1985 and won European Footballer of the Year awards in 1983, 1984, and 1985.

$2,500-4,000

99
DAVID BECKHAM 2009 A.C. MILAN MATCH WORN JERSEY
An Adidas brand long-sleeve A.C. Milan away jersey match worn by David Beckham during the 2009-2010 season. Affixed to the right sleeve is the logo patch for the top flight of Italian football, Serie A. Affixed to the left sleeve is the UEFA Champions League trophy patch, with the number 7 representing A.C. Milan's seven league championships.

$400-600

100
KAKÁ 2005 A.C. MILAN MATCH WORN JERSEY

An Adidas brand away jersey match worn during the 2005-2006 season by then A.C. Milan team member Ricardo Izecson dos Santos Leite, known simply as Kaká. The white jersey features red and black striping and the A.C. Milan, Italian flag, Adidas, and Opel emblems on the front with a UEFA Champions League Trophy 6 emblem on the left sleeve. On the back of the jersey is "Kaká" lettering above his number 22.

$600-800

101
CAFU 2005 A.C. MILAN CHAMPIONS LEAGUE MATCH WORN JERSEY

An Adidas brand Champions League jersey match worn during the 2005-2006 season by then A.C. Milan team member Marcos Evangelista de Morais, known simply as Cafu. The red and black striped jersey features A.C. Milan, Adidas, and Zafira emblems on the front with additional UEFA Champions League and UEFA Champions League Trophy 6 emblems on the sleeves. On the back of the jersey is embroidered A.C. Milan lettering over "Cafu" and his number 2.

$400-600

102
RONALDINHO 2002 PARIS SAINT-GERMAIN FC MATCH WORN JERSEY

A Nike brand home jersey match worn during the 2002-2003 season by then Paris Saint-Germain Football Club team member Ronaldo de Assis Moreira, known simply as Ronaldinho. The blue jersey features red and white striping and a Nike logo, Paris Saint-Germain FC emblem, and Thomson logo on the front. On the back of the jersey is "Ronaldinho" lettering above a number 10 with inset LFP (Liga de Fútbol Profesional or La Liga) logos.

$600-800

103
2016 SEVILLA FC PLAYER'S UEFA EUROPA LEAGUE TROPHY

A 2016 Sevilla football club player's UEFA Europa League trophy, given to a Sevilla player on the team that defeated Liverpool 3-1 in the 2016 Europa League final to win Sevilla's third consecutive Europa League trophy. The trophy is housed in its original red case.

Case, 13 by 7 7/16 by 4 1/2 inches

$600-800

104
1982 FC BARCELONA MATCH WORN JERSEY
A Meyba brand long-sleeve FC Barcelona home jersey match worn during the 1981-1982 season. Barcelona won the 1982 European Cup Winners' Cup Final, defeating Standard Liège of Belgium on May 12 on Barcelona's home ground, Camp Nou in Barcelona, Spain. Barcelona won the match 2-1. Size G.

$400-600

105
LIONEL MESSI MATCH WORN 2010-2011 FC BARCELONA JERSEY
A Nike brand FC Barcelona away football jersey match worn by Lionel Messi during the 2010-2011 Spanish La Liga season. The jersey features the FC Barcelona logo stitched on the upper left chest with the inside back of the logo presenting the motto "Tots Units Fem Força" (United we are strong). Also appearing on the jersey is the FIFA Club World Champions logo, representing the FIFA Club Championship Barcelona won in 2009. The back of the jersey features Messi's name in thermally applied lettering above his uniform number 10. An LFP (Liga de Fútbol Profesional or La Liga) logo patch is applied to the right sleeve of the jersey, and a TV 3 club sponsor logo is applied to the left sleeve above the club's motto, "més que un club" (more than a club). Accompanied by a certificate of authenticity from 100% Authentic. Size M.

$1,500-2,500

106
2011 FC BARCELONA TEAM ISSUED AND SIGNED JERSEY
A Nike brand FC Barcelona team issued jersey signed by 16 members of Barça who played for the team in 2011 including Piqué, Puyol, Xavi, Iniesta, Messi, Pinto, Busquets, Pedro, Maxwell, Afellay, Adriano, and Fontàs. One of the 16 signatures is on the back of the jersey. The front upper left of the jersey features the FC Barcelona logo. At the center of the jersey is the Qatar Foundation logo. On the back of the jersey are the "FCB" initials and the red and yellow bars representing Barcelona and Catalonia and the UNICEF logo. On the interior collar is the club motto, "més que un club" (more than a club). Size M.

$600-800

107
LIONEL MESSI SIGNED FC BARCELONA CAPTAIN'S ARMBAND
An FC Barcelona captain's armband signed by Lionel Messi in black marker to the left of the Barça logo. Below the signature and logo is "Capità" ("Captain" in Catalan). The armband is accompanied by a letter of authenticity for the signature from JSA.

$200-400

108

DAVID VILLA FC BARCELONA 2011 MATCH WORN JERSEY

A Nike brand FC Barcelona jersey match worn by David Villa during the Spanish Super Cup match between Barcelona and Real Madrid at the Camp Nou stadium in Barcelona on August 17, 2011. Barcelona won the Spanish Super Cup 3-2. The front upper left of the jersey features the FC Barcelona logo. Centered on the jersey is the Qatar Foundation sponsor logo. Applied to the back of the jersey is "David Villa" above his uniform number 7, with the UNICEF charity logo applied to the lower back. An LFP (Liga de Fútbol Profesional or La Liga) logo patch has been applied to the right sleeve of the jersey, with the TV3 club sponsor logo applied to the left sleeve. Size M.

$400-600

109

MARIANO GARCÍA REMÓN SIGNED 1980S REAL MADRID MATCH WORN JERSEY

An Adidas brand long-sleeve Real Madrid jersey match worn by Mariano García Remón during the 1980s and signed by him on the front of the jersey in black marker. Including his youth career, he spent 20 years with Real Madrid, from 1966-1986. The jersey features Real Madrid's first-time sponsor, Zanussi. It is accompanied by a signed letter from García Remón stating "I certify that the Real Madrid jersey with the number 1 was used by me in a game in the 80s and comes from my private collection of shirts that were given to me by other players." Size M.

$800-1,200

110

SÁVIO 2000 REAL MADRID MATCH WORN JERSEY

An Adidas brand Real Madrid home jersey match worn by Sávio Bortolini Pimentel, known simply as Sávio, during the 2000-2001 preseason. Joining Real Madrid in 1998, he was part of the team that won three UEFA Champions League titles and the 2001 national championship. The front upper left of the jersey features the Real Madrid logo. Applied to the back of the jersey are "Savio" and his number 11 in black lettering and numbering. The jersey is accompanied by a certificate of authenticity from Prorrogação Comércio de Artigos Esportivos LTDA. Size XL.

$600-800

111

DAVID BECKHAM 2005 REAL MADRID MATCH WORN JERSEY

An Adidas brand long-sleeve Real Madrid away jersey match worn by legendary English footballer David Beckham during the 2004-2005 season. The front upper left of the jersey features the Real Madrid logo. On the right sleeve is the LFP logo of the Liga de Fútbol Profesional or La Liga, the sports association responsible for Spain's professional football leagues. Applied to the back of the jersey are "Beckham" and his number 23 in white-on-black lettering and numbering. The jersey is accompanied by a certificate of authenticity from Prorrogação Comércio de Artigos Esportivos LTDA. Size L.

$800-1,200

112
RONALDO LUÍS NAZÁRIO DE LIMA 2005 REAL MADRID MATCH WORN JERSEY
An Adidas brand long-sleeve Real Madrid home jersey match worn by Ronaldo Luís Nazário de Lima, known simply as Ronaldo, during the 2005-2006 season. Ronaldo is a three-time FIFA World Player of the Year and two-time Ballon d'Or recipient. The front upper left of the jersey features the Real Madrid logo. On the right sleeve is the UEFA Champions League logo patch. On the left sleeve is the UEFA Champions League trophy patch, with the number 9 representing Real Madrid's then nine league championships. Applied to the back of the jersey are "Ronaldo" and his number 9 in black-on-silver lettering and numbering. The jersey is accompanied by a certificate of authenticity from Prorrogação Comércio de Artigos Esportivos LTDA. Size L.

$800-1,200

113
RONALDO LUÍS NAZÁRIO DE LIMA 2006 REAL MADRID MATCH WORN JERSEY
An Adidas brand Real Madrid away jersey match worn by Ronaldo Luís Nazário de Lima, known simply as Ronaldo, during the 2006-2007 season. Ronaldo is a three-time FIFA World Player of the Year and two-time Ballon d'Or recipient. The front upper left of the jersey features the Real Madrid logo. On the upper right is the patch symbolizing Real Madrid's "FIFA Award Best Club XX Century." On the right sleeve is the LFP logo of the Liga de Fútbol Profesional or La Liga, the sports association responsible for Spain's professional football leagues. Applied to the back of the jersey are "Ronaldo" and his number 9 in white-on-silver lettering and numbering. Size L.

$800-1,200

114
MARCELO 2008 REAL MADRID MATCH WORN JERSEY
An Adidas brand Real Madrid jersey match worn during the 2008-2009 season by Marcelo Vieira da Silva Júnior, known simply as Marcelo. The jersey features the Real Madrid C.F. emblem and bwin.com logo on the front, with an LFP (Liga de Fútbol Profesional or La Liga) emblem on the right sleeve. On the back of the jersey are "Marcelo" and his uniform number 12. Size L.

$400-600

115
XABI ALONSO REAL MADRID MATCH WORN JERSEY
An Adidas brand Real Madrid jersey match worn by Xabi Alonso, who played for Real Madrid from 2009 to 2014. The front upper left of the jersey features the Real Madrid logo. At the center is the bwin main sponsor logo. On the right sleeve is the UEFA Champions League logo patch. On the left sleeve is the UEFA Champions League trophy patch, with the number 9 representing Real Madrid's then nine league championships, and the UEFA Respect patch. On the back of the jersey are "Alonso" and his number 14 in white lettering and numbering.

$600-800

116
CRISTIANO RONALDO 2014 REAL MADRID MATCH ISSUED JERSEY
An Adidas brand long-sleeve Real Madrid away jersey issued to Cristiano Ronaldo for the May 7, 2014, match between Real Madrid and Real Valladolid. The match ended in a 1-1 draw. The front upper left of the jersey features the Real Madrid logo. On the right sleeve is the LFP logo of the Liga de Fútbol Profesional or La Liga, the sports association responsible for Spain's professional football leagues. Applied to the back of the jersey are "Ronaldo" and his number 7 in black lettering and numbering. The jersey is accompanied by a certificate of authenticity from the Football Museum Madrid. Size 10.

$400-600

117
1896 ATHENS OLYMPICS
PARTICIPATION MEDAL WITH CASE
An 1896 Athens Olympics participation medal featuring a seated Nike holding a laurel wreath over a phoenix rising from flames with the Acropolis in the background. On the other side is Greek legend denoting the 1896 Olympic Games, the first modern Olympics Games. At the bottom edge is "W. Pittner Wien," for Pittner, the medal manufacturer of Vienna, Austria. The medal is housed in its original case.

Diameter, 2 1/4 inches

$800-1,200

118
1900 PARIS OLYMPICS SILVER WINNER'S MEDAL

A silver winner's medal for "Concours D'Exercices Militaires Preparatoires" in the 1900 Paris Olympics, which took place during the Exposition Universelle Internationale de 1900, the

World's Fair held in Paris in 1900 to celebrate the new century. The plaquette medal features a relief figure of a victorious athlete on one side and a winged Nike victory figure on the other side. Stamped on the bottom rim of the medal is the cornucopia symbol and the text "Argent" (silver).

2 3/8 by 1 5/8 inches

$1,500-2,000

119
1900 PARIS OLYMPICS UNION OF FRENCH SHOOTING SOCIETIES MEDAL

A silver award medal presented by the Union des Sociétés de Tir de France (Union of Shooting Societies of France) during the 1900 Paris Olympics, which took place during the Exposition Universelle Internationale de 1900, the World's Fair held

in Paris in 1900 to celebrate the new century. The medal features Victory rising, carrying an armed man with "Honneur Patrie" (Honor Country). The text on the other side identifies the medal's association with the "Concours International de L'Exposition 1900." Stamped on the rim of the medal is the cornucopia symbol and the text "Argent" (silver).

Diameter, 1 3/4 inches

$400-600

120
1900 PARIS OLYMPICS SILVER WINNER'S MEDAL

A silver winner's medal for "Exercices Physiques Et Sports" in the 1900 Paris Olympics, which took place during the Exposition Universelle Internationale de 1900, the World's Fair held in Paris in 1900 to celebrate the new century. The plaquette medal features a relief figure of a victorious athlete on one side and a winged Nike victory figure on the other. Stamped on the bottom rim of the medal is the cornucopia symbol and the text "Argent" (silver).

2 3/8 by 1 5/8 inches

$2,000-4,000

121
1900 PARIS OLYMPICS SILVER AWARD MEDAL

A silver award medal from the 1900 Paris Olympics, which took place during the Exposition Universelle Internationale de 1900, the World's Fair held in Paris in 1900 to celebrate the new century. One side features the words "Republique Francaise" around an image of Marianne, a national symbol of the French Republic, an allegory of liberty and reason, and a Paris skyline. The other side is a winged Nike victory figure supporting an athlete who holds a torch to the sky. "Exposition Universelle Internationale" rings the edge of the medal, with "1900" above the Nike figure on the right. The rim of the medal is stamped with the cornucopia symbol and the word "Bronze."

Diameter, 2 1/2 inches

$600-800

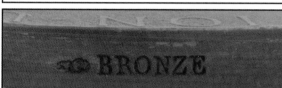

122
1900 PARIS OLYMPICS BRONZE MEDAL WITH CASE

A bronze medal from the 1900 Paris Olympics, which took place during the Exposition Universelle Internationale de 1900, the World's Fair held in Paris in 1900 to celebrate the new century. One side features the words "Republique Francaise" around an image of Marianne, a national symbol of the French Republic, an allegory of liberty and reason, and a Paris skyline. On the other side is a winged Nike victory figure supporting an athlete who holds a torch to the sky. "Exposition Universelle Internationale" rings the edge of the medal, with "1900" above the Nike figure on the right. The rim of the medal is stamped with the cornucopia symbol and the word "Bronze." The medal is housed in its original case.

Case, 3 1/4 by 3 1/4 inches

$400-600

123
1912 STOCKHOLM OLYMPICS SILVER WINNER'S MEDAL

A 1912 Stockholm Olympics silver winner's medal featuring two female figures crowning a victorious Olympic athlete with a laurel wreath and the stamps "Vaughtons" and "BM." On the other side is the text "Olympiska Spelen Stockholm 1912" with the figure of a herald proclaiming the Olympic Games and standing before a bust of Per Henrik Ling, the founder of the Swedish gymnastics system. Taking place between May 5 and July 22, 1912, the Stockholm Olympics featured over 2,400 athletes, almost 50 of them women, from 28 countries competing in 102 events in 14 sports.

Diameter, 1 5/16 inches

$6,000-8,000

124
1912 STOCKHOLM OLYMPICS GOLD WINNER'S MEDAL WITH PLAQUE

A 1912 Stockholm Olympics gold winner's medal won by Gaston Salmon, a Belgian épée, foil, and saber fencer. Salmon competed for Belgium in three events, winning this gold medal in team épée. The medal is gilt silver and features two female figures crowning a victorious Olympic athlete with a laurel wreath and the stamps "Vaughtons" and "B.M." On the other side is the text "Olympiska Spelen Stockholm 1912" with the figure of a herald proclaiming the Olympic Games and standing before a bust of Ling, the founder of the Swedish gymnastics system. The medal is accompanied by a plaque from Brussels' French Chamber of Commerce, issued in August 1935 in "Reconnaiffance" (gratitude) declaring Salmon a Knight of the Legion of Honor.

Medal diameter, 1 3/8 inches; Plaque, 4 3/4 by 3 1/4 inches

$10,000-20,000

125
1920 ANTWERP OLYMPICS PARTICIPATION MEDAL
A 1920 Antwerp Olympics participation medal featuring Nike crowning three victorious athletes and Flying Victory crowning a charioteer. Antwerp, Belgium, hosted the seventh modern Olympic Games with 29 national teams competing in 24 sports. The first modern games took place in 1896 in Athens, Greece.

Diameter, 2 3/8 inches

$600-800

126
1920 ANTWERP OLYMPICS SILVER WINNER'S MEDAL
A 1920 Antwerp Olympics silver winner's medal featuring on one side a victorious athlete bringing back the palm of victory, and on the other side an Antwerp monument standing before the cathedral and port of Antwerp. Stamped on the rim of the medal is the letter "A."

Diameter, 2 3/8 inches

$4,000-6,000

127
1936 GARMISCH OLYMPICS PARTICIPATION MEDAL

A 1936 Garmisch-Partenkirchen Winter Olympics participation medal, featuring the Olympic rings with a stylized image of the mountains of Garmisch-Partenkirchen, Germany, and the Olympics motto "Citius Altius Fortius" (Faster Higher Stronger). These Winter Games in Garmisch-Partenkirchen were the fourth Winter Games and the first to include Alpine skiing events.

Diameter, 2 3/8 inches

$800-1,200

128
1936 BERLIN OLYMPICS PARTICIPATION MEDAL WITH CASE

A 1936 Berlin Olympics participation medal featuring five athletes pulling the ropes of the Olympic bell on one side and the Olympic bell embossed with the German eagle on the other side. At the edge of the medal is the name of Otto Placzek, the Berlin sculptor who designed the medal. Stamped on the rim of the medal is "H. Noack Berlin," one of four foundries that produced the 1936 Berlin Olympics Participation Medals.

Diameter, 3 inches

$400-600

129
1948 ST. MORITZ OLYMPICS PARTICIPATION MEDAL
A 1948 St. Moritz Winter Olympics participation medal featuring Olympic rings over the text "Vmes Jeux Olympiques D'Hiver St. Moritz 1948" surrounded by snowflakes on one side and the Nike figure with mountains in the background on the other side. The St. Moritz Winter Olympics were the first Olympic Games since 1936 and the end of World War II.

Diameter, 1 9/16 inches

$600-800

130
1960 SQUAW VALLEY OLYMPICS PARTICIPATION MEDAL
A 1960 Squaw Valley Winter Olympics participation medal featuring the Squaw Valley Olympics logo with the Olympic rings and "VIII Olympic Winter Games" around the edge on one side and the Olympic torch with "Squaw Valley, California 1960" on the other side. Stamped on the rim is "HJCO.," designating the medal designer, Herff Jones Co.

Diameter, 1 7/8 inches

$800-1,000

131
1968 GRENOBLE OLYMPICS PARTICIPATION MEDAL WITH CASE
A 1968 Grenoble Winter Olympics participation medal featuring a Greek style head of an athlete surrounded by snowflakes and the stamp of the manufacturer, J.M. Coeffin, on one side and a cityscape of Grenoble, France, with the Olympics rings and text marking the 10th Winter Olympic Games on the other side. The rim of the medal is stamped with the cornucopia symbol and "Bronze." It is housed in its original case.

Diameter, 3 inches

$200-400

132
1972 MUNICH OLYMPICS PARTICIPATION MEDAL
A 1972 Munich Olympics participation medal encased in a clear acrylic square, featuring the Munich Olympic emblem, a wreath of rays with superimposed spiral, and the Olympic rings over two hands, one holding a stylized olive branch. On the base of the acrylic case is a label stating the medal is stainless steel, designed by Fritz Koenig and embossed by Preissler of Pforzheim, Germany.

3 by 3 inches

$300-400

133
1980 LAKE PLACID OLYMPICS PARTICIPATION MEDAL WITH CASE
A 1980 Lake Placid Winter Olympics participation medal featuring a collage of competitive athletes from various sports and the Lake Placid Olympics logo surrounded by the Olympic oath. The medal is housed in its original case.

Case, 4 1/8 by 4 1/8 inches

$400-600

134
1996 ATLANTA OLYMPICS PARTICIPATION MEDAL WITH CASE
A 1996 Atlanta Olympics participation medal featuring the Atlanta 1996 Olympic torch and rings logo and a stylized quilt of leaves with the text "Centennial Olympic Games" marking the 100th anniversary of the first modern Olympic Games in Athens, Greece, in 1896. The medal is housed in its original pouch and box.

Box, 3 7/16 by 3 7/16 inches

$200-400

135
2016 RIO OLYMPICS PARTICIPATION MEDAL WITH CERTIFICATE AND PASS
A 2016 Rio Olympic Games Official participation medal, issued by the International Olympic Committee, in its original case. The pebble-shaped copper medal with nickel flash features "XXXI Olympiad Rio 2016" in English, French, and Portuguese and the Olympic rings on the obverse. On reverse are the emblem of the Rio Games, "Rio2016," and the Olympic rings. The 2016 Summer Olympics took place in Rio de Janeiro, Brazil, August 5-21. Accompanying the medal are a participation certificate and an Olympic Closing Ceremony marching pass.

Case, 5 1/2 by 3 3/4 inches

$300-500

136
2012 LONDON OLYMPICS USED RELAY TORCH
A 2012 London Summer Olympics relay torch used during the pre-Olympics torch relay that was run from May 19 through July 27, passing through the United Kingdom, Jersey, Guernsey, the Isle of Man, and the Republic of Ireland. The torch was designed by East London design company Barber & Osgerby. The 8,000 cutout circles represent each of the torchbearers. The circles run the length of the torch, so the burner system that keeps the Olympic flame alive can be seen. The triangular shape of the torch was inspired by a series of "threes" that are found in Olympic Games history: the Olympic values of respect, excellence, and friendship; the Olympic motto of faster, higher, stronger; the fact that Great Britain hosted the Olympics in 1908, 1948, and 2012; and the vision for the 2012 London Games to combine sport, education, and culture. The torch is the color of gold to reflect the Olympic flame's brightness, warmth, and the light that it shines.

Length, 31 1/2 inches

$4,000-6,000

137
EVANDER HOLYFIELD VS. HASIM RAHMAN FIGHT WORN ROBE

A red terrycloth robe worn by Evander Holyfield for his fight against Hasim Rahman on June 1, 2002, at the Boardwalk Hall in Atlantic City, New Jersey. The robe features red acetate satin lapels and cuffs, with Holyfield Warrior logos on both sides of the upper front, as well as a larger logo on the upper back. Surrounding the base of the robe is an embroidered wide strip of red satin with the verse "I can do all things through Christ who strengthens me" appearing in silver lettering and "Overcome/ Evander/ Real Deal/ Holyfield/ Warrior..." in various colors. Holyfield would win the bout against Rahman on a technical decision when the referee stopped the fight after the eighth round due to "an unusually large swelling" over Rahman's eye.

$2,000-4,000

138
MUHAMMAD ALI AND JOE FRAZIER SIGNED "THRILLA IN MANILA" CLOSED CIRCUIT POSTER

An original poster advertising the closed circuit broadcast of Muhammad Ali's third fight vs. Joe Frazier, dubbed the "Thrilla in Manila," which took place at the Araneta Coliseum in Barangay Cubao, Quezon City, Metro Manila, Philippines, on Tuesday, September 30, 1975. The poster features images from an original artwork by LeRoy Neiman and states that the fight will be shown on September 30 at The Omni. Ali and Frazier have signed the poster in black marker. Ali won the fight with a technical knockout in the 14th round and retained his WBC Heavyweight championship title. Accompanied by a letter of authenticity from JSA.

22 by 14 inches

$1,000-2,000

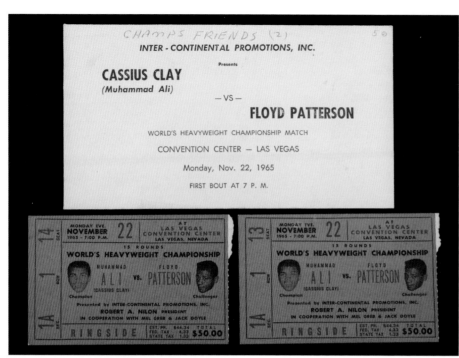

139
MUHAMMAD ALI VS. FLOYD PATTERSON
1965 FIGHT TICKET STUBS PAIR WITH ENVELOPE

A pair of ringside, front row ticket stubs to the Muhammad Ali (Cassius Clay) vs. Floyd Patterson World Heavyweight Championship fight on November 22, 1965, at the Las Vegas Convention Center. Ali won the fight through technical knockout. The ticket stubs are from the collection of Betty Griffin, a friend of Ali's in Los Angeles. They are accompanied by the envelope for the tickets, which is marked "Champs Friends (2)" in blue ink, a September 1963 photo of Ali with Griffin, and a February 13, 1976, issue of the San Juan Diary Journal with Ali on the cover and the autograph and inscription "Good Luck/ Jack Dempsey" that Ali got from Dempsey for Griffin. There is also a certificate of authenticity for the Dempsey signature from JSA.

Magazine, 10 3/4 by 8 1/2 inches

$800-1,200

140
MUHAMMAD ALI SIGNED
BOXING GLOVES PAIR

A pair of Everlast brand boxing gloves, the right glove signed by Muhammad Ali in black marker. Size 14. The autographed glove is accompanied by a letter of authenticity from Stacks of Plaques and a certificate of authenticity from Todd Mueller Autographs.

Length, each glove, 11 1/4 inches

$800-1,200

141
MUHAMMAD ALI AKA CASSIUS CLAY AND JOE FRAZIER SIGNED BOXING TRUNKS

A pair of white satin Everlast brand boxing trunks with black trim signed by Muhammad Ali and Joe Frazier in blue marker. Ali's signature reads "Muhammad Ali/ AKA/ Cassius Clay." The trunks are accompanied by a certificate of registration from Online Authentics. Size L.

$1,000-2,000

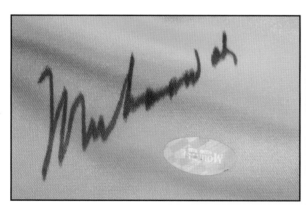

142
MUHAMMAD ALI SIGNED HANDPAINTED ROBE

A white satin Everlast brand robe with black trim signed by Muhammad Ali in black marker. The robe features a handpainted image depicting Ali standing over Sonny Liston after his first-round knockout of Liston during the 1965 World Heavyweight title fight at St. Dominic's Arena in Lewiston, Maine, on May 25, 1965. The robe is accompanied by a certificate of authenticity from Mounted Memories. Size XL.

$1,000-2,000

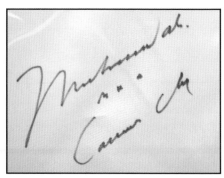

143
MUHAMMAD ALI AKA CASSIUS CLAY SIGNED BOXING TRUNKS
A pair of white satin Everlast brand boxing trunks with black trim signed by Muhammad Ali "Muhammad Ali/ AKA/ Cassius Clay" in black marker. The trunks are accompanied by a letter of authenticity from PSA/DNA. Size XL.

$1,000-2,000

144
1938 SAMMY STEIN LIGHTWEIGHT CHAMPION OF THE WORLD BELT
A 1938 Lightweight Champion of the World belt presented to Sammy Stein, the winner of the World Lightweight Wrestling Championship in November 1938 in Mexico, when he defeated Mexican wrestler El Lobo Negro at the Lucha Libre Arena in Mexico City. The belt features silver and brass medallions with the central medallion depicting two wrestlers. The other medallions identify "Young Sammy Stein USA" as the "Lightweight Champion of the World 1938." The belt is housed in a wood and glass display case. It is accompanied by a photograph of Stein wearing the belt and a March 1986 *Ring Arts* magazine with an article about Stein.

Case, 21 5/8 by 9 7/8 by 7 1/8 inches

$6,000-8,000

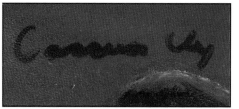

145
MUHAMMAD ALI CASSIUS CLAY SIGNED BOXING GLOVE WITH ARTWORK

A red right-hand Everlast brand boxing glove signed "Cassius Clay" by Muhammad Ali in black marker above a handpainted image of the boxer. Accompanied by a letter of authenticity from PSA/DNA.

Length, 12 inches

$800-1,200

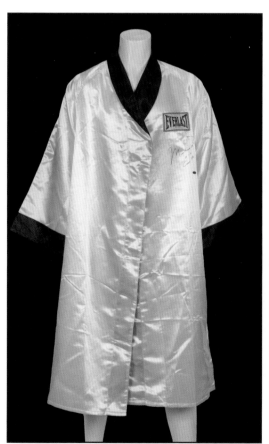

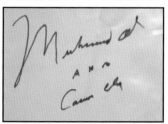

146
MUHAMMAD ALI AKA CASSIUS CLAY SIGNED ROBE

A white satin Everlast brand robe with black trim signed by Muhammad Ali "Muhammad Ali/ AKA/ Cassius Clay" in black marker. The robe is accompanied by a certificate of authenticity from Steiner Sports.

$800-1,200

147
MUHAMMAD ALI AND JOE FRAZIER SIGNED ORIGINAL 1971 CLOSED CIRCUIT FIGHT POSTER

An original poster for the closed circuit broadcast of the "Battle of the Champions" between Muhammad Ali and Joe Frazier that took place at Madison Square Garden in New York City on March 8, 1971. This fight is more widely known as "The Fight of the Century," as it was marketed leading up to the event, and was the first of three fights between Ali and Frazier in their careers. Ali and Frazier have both signed the poster in black marker. Frazier would go on to win the fight by unanimous decision after fighting the full scheduled 15 rounds. The poster is accompanied by a letter of authenticity for the signatures from PSA/DNA.

22 by 14 inches

$3,000-5,000

148
MUHAMMAD ALI AKA CASSIUS CLAY SIGNED BOXING GLOVE

A red right-hand Everlast brand boxing glove signed by Muhammad Ali "Muhammad Ali/ AKA/ Cassius Clay" in black marker. Accompanied by a letter of authenticity from PSA/DNA.

Length, 12 inches

$800-1,200

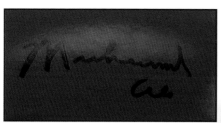

149
MUHAMMAD ALI AND OTHERS MULTI-SIGNED BOXING GLOVE

A red right-hand Everlast brand boxing glove signed by Muhammad Ali in black marker and featuring the signatures of Featherweight and Super Featherweight champion Sandy Saddler, Lightweight and Light Welterweight champion Carlos Ortiz, two-time world Heavyweight champion Floyd Patterson, and Sugar Ray Leonard, who won world titles in five weight divisions. Accompanied by a letter of authenticity for the signatures from JSA.

Length, 12 inches

$600-800

150
MUHAMMAD ALI CASSIUS CLAY SIGNED HANDPAINTED BOXING TRUNKS

A pair of white satin Everlast brand boxing trunks with black trim signed "Cassius Clay" by Muhammad Ali in black marker. A handpainted image on the trunks depicts a youthful Cassius Clay. The trunks are accompanied by a letter of authenticity from PSA/DNA. Size M.

$800-1,200

151
MUHAMMAD ALI "THE GREATEST" AND ERNIE TERRELL SIGNED GRADED BOXING TRUNKS

A pair of white satin Everlast brand boxing trunks with red trim signed by Muhammad Ali and Heavyweight champion Ernie Terrell in black marker. Ali has inscribed his signature with "The Greatest." Ali defeated Terrell in a 15-round bout on February 6, 1967, at the Astrodome in Houston to retain his Heavyweight title. Both signatures are graded by Alico LLC/Steve Jackson a 10 out of 10. Accompanied by a letter of authenticity for each signature from Alico LLC/Steve Jackson. Size XXL.

$1,000-2,000

152
MUHAMMAD ALI SIGNED GICLÉE CANVAS IMAGE

A large color, limited edition giclée image on canvas of Muhammad Ali by Joe Petruccio. The image is signed by Ali in gold paint pen. The canvas is accompanied by a certificate of authenticity for the Ali signature from PSA/DNA.

50 by 34 inches

$1,000-2,000

153
MUHAMMAD ALI VS. TREVOR BERBICK TRAINING WORN AND SIGNED BOXING TRUNKS
A pair of black velvet Everlast brand trunks with light gold color trim worn by Muhammad Ali during training sessions for the final fight of his professional career vs. Trevor Berbick. The fight, billed as "Drama in Bahama," took place on December 11, 1981, at Queen Elizabeth Sports Centre, Nassau, Bahamas. Ali would lose the fight by unanimous decision after fighting the full 10 rounds. The trunks are signed by Ali on the front left in gold marker. They are accompanied by certificates of authenticity from Craig Hamilton/Jo Sports Inc., Grey Flannel, and JSA for the signature.

$4,000-6,000

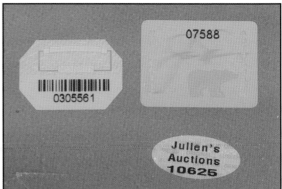

154
MUHAMMAD ALI AND JACK NICKLAUS SIGNED PHOTOGRAPH

A large color print of a photograph of Muhammad Ali and golfer Jack Nicklaus, signed by Ali and Nicklaus in black marker. The photograph was taken at the 1996 PGA Championship at the Valhalla Golf Club in Louisville, Kentucky, where Nicklaus received the *Sports Illustrated* Muhammad Ali Legacy Award. The award honors athletes and sports figures who have embodied sportsmanship, leadership, and philanthropy. In 1996, the award was renamed the *Sports Illustrated* Muhammad Ali Legacy Award in tribute to Ali the boxer and humanitarian. Affixed to the photograph are Mounted Memories and Jack Nicklaus Authentic holograms. No certificates present.

20 by 16 inches

$600-800

155
MUHAMMAD ALI SIGNED 1996 OLYMPICS TORCH PHOTOGRAPH

A large color print of a photograph of Muhammad Ali, originally taken on the night of the opening ceremony of the 1996 Summer Olympics in Atlanta. The photograph depicts Ali holding the Olympic torch and is signed "Muhammad Ali" in silver marker. Ali had the honor of being the last member of the 1996 Olympic Torch Relay, thus lighting the Olympic flame at the opening ceremony of the Olympic Games at Centennial Olympic Stadium in Atlanta on July 19, 1996, marking the official opening of the Games. Accompanied by a hologram from Ali Enterprises and a certificate of authenticity label from PSA/DNA.

20 by 16 inches

$400-600

156
MIKE TYSON SIGNED
COLLAGE ORIGINAL OIL PAINTING

An original oil painting on canvas from Koestler Award-winning portrait artist Glen Folan (British, b. 1986) featuring a collage of three images of Heavyweight champion boxer Mike Tyson. The painting is signed by the artist in the bottom right. Tyson has signed the painting in silver paint pen in the lower left. The painting is accompanied by an image of Tyson signing the painting.

59 by 39 1/2 inches

$1,000-2,000

157
MIKE TYSON SIGNED
IN-ACTION ORIGINAL
OIL PAINTING

An original oil painting on canvas from Koestler Award-winning portrait artist Glen Folan (British, b. 1986) depicting Heavyweight champion boxer Mike Tyson in action throwing a punch against Reggie Gross during their June 13, 1986, fight at Madison Square Garden in New York City. Tyson won by a technical knockout in round one. The painting is signed by the artist in the bottom left. Tyson has signed the painting in silver paint pen in the upper right.

59 by 39 1/2 inches

$1,000-2,000

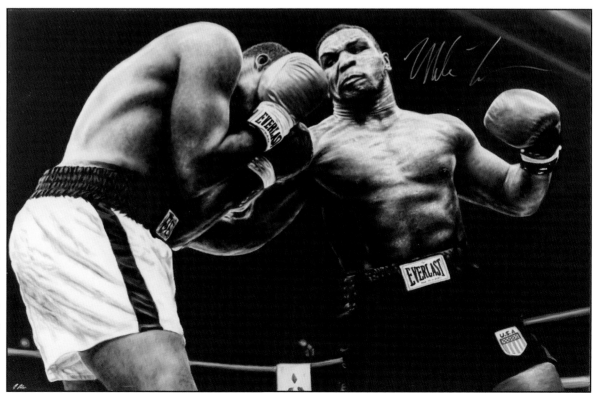

158
MAYWEATHER AND McGREGOR
SIGNED BOXING GLOVE

An Everlast brand right-hand boxing glove signed by Floyd Mayweather and Conor McGregor in silver marker. The glove includes a Beckett Witness label and a PSA/DNA label for the signatures and a Beckett certificate of authenticity.

Length, 11 1/4 inches

$600-800

159
CONOR McGREGOR
SIGNED UFC GLOVES PAIR

A pair of UFC gloves, each glove signed by Conor McGregor in silver marker. In his August 2017 bout with Floyd Mayweather, Mayweather won by technical knockout. Each glove is accompanied by a certificate of authenticity for the signature from PSA/DNA.

Length, each glove, 11 inches

$400-600

160
CONOR McGREGOR SIGNED MMA SET
An Everlast brand MMA set of two mitts and one pad, each item signed by mixed martial artist and professional boxer Conor McGregor in silver marker. Each mitt and the pad include a PSA/DNA certificate of authenticity for the signatures.

Pad, 10 3/4 by 8 1/2 inches; Length, each mitt, 9 1/2 inches

$600-800

161
CONOR McGREGOR SIGNED UFC SET
A UFC set of two gloves and one pad, each item signed by mixed martial artist and professional boxer Conor McGregor in silver marker. Each glove and the pad have a certificate of authenticity for the signature from PSA/DNA.

Pad, 7 1/8 by 7 inches; Length, each mitt, 8 1/8 inches

$600-800

162
MAYWEATHER AND McGREGOR SIGNED BOXING GLOVE
An Everlast brand right-hand boxing glove signed by Floyd Mayweather and Conor McGregor in silver marker. The glove includes a Beckett Witness label and a PSA/DNA label for the signatures and a Beckett certificate of authenticity.

Length, 12 1/2 inches

$600-800

163
CONOR McGREGOR SIGNED PHOTOGRAPHS GROUP
A group of five large color prints of a photograph of mixed martial artist and professional boxer Conor McGregor, each one signed by McGregor in silver marker. Each photo features a PSA/DNA certificate of authenticity label for the signature.

19 3/4 by 15 3/4 inches, each

$400-600

164
CONOR McGREGOR SIGNED BOXING GLOVES PAIR
A pair of Everlast brand Evershield boxing gloves, each one signed by Conor McGregor in black marker. Each glove comes with a certificate of authenticity for the signature from PSA/DNA.

Length, each glove, 11 3/4 inches

$400-600

165
MUHAMMAD ALI 1976 TRAINING-WORN FIGHT ROBE
A white terrycloth robe with satin letters on the back spelling out "Muhammad Ali" worn by Ali while training for his third fight with Ken Norton. That fight took place on September 28, 1976, and was the last championship fight ever held at Yankee Stadium. Norton had broken Ali's jaw and beaten Ali in their first fight. Ali avenged that loss in their second fight. This fight was to be the rubber game of the match. Although Norton appeared to be leading for most of the fight, Ali finished strong to win the judges' decision. In the week leading up to the fight, Ali stayed at the New York City home of prominent fight promoter Harold Conrad to avoid the media onslaught. Ali gave the robe to Conrad at that time. Conrad later passed the robe on to his son. The label inside the robe indicates that it was "Made Exclusively for Muhammad Ali" by Everlast.

$15,000-20,000

NOV. 3, 2017 I LOS ANGELES, CA

BIDDER REGISTRATION FORM

Julien's Auctions invites you to complete and submit this Bidder Registration Form. You acknowledge your proposed registration to bid in the above-identified Auction is subject to verification of the information that you provide, and approval of your registration is at the sole and complete discretion of Julien's Auctions. We will provide you with written confirmation if and when your application is approved.

This auction sale will be conducted in accordance with Julien's Auctions' Auction Terms and Conditions ("Terms and Conditions") in the form set out in our auction catalogue, which are incorporated herein by reference. You should read the Auction Terms and Conditions which describe the charges payable by you on the purchases you make and other terms relating to bidding and buying at the auction, which you accept by signing this form. You should ask us any questions you have about the Terms and Conditions before signing this Bidder Registration Form.

PLEASE CHECK **ONE** OF THE FOLLOWING:

☐ I will be attending the live auction
☐ I will be placing absentee bids
☐ I will be phone bidding

Name: _____ Company: _____

Email: _____

Address: _____

City: _____ State/Provence: _____

ZIP/Postal Code: _____ Country: _____

Day Phone: _____ Cell Phone: _____ Fax: _____

☐ Check here if different billing address

☐ Absentee Bid(s)   ☐ Phone Bid(s)

Please state your MAXIMUM Absentee bid in United States dollars (USD$) for each Lot
(excluding Buyer's Premium, Online Fee, taxes, shipping fees or other charges):

Lot #:_____ Bid:_____   Lot #:_____ Bid:_____   Lot #:_____ Bid:_____   Lot #:_____ Bid:_____

Lot #:_____ Bid:_____   Lot #:_____ Bid:_____   Lot #:_____ Bid:_____   Lot #:_____ Bid:_____

Lot #:_____ Bid:_____   Lot #:_____ Bid:_____   Lot #:_____ Bid:_____   Lot #:_____ Bid:_____

Lot #:_____ Bid:_____   Lot #:_____ Bid:_____   Lot #:_____ Bid:_____   Lot #:_____ Bid:_____

Bidder Registration Form continued

Billing Address (if different than previous page):

Name: _____

Address:_____

City: _____ State/Provence: _____

ZIP/Postal Code: _____ Country: _____

Type of Credit Card:

☐ Visa ☐ MasterCard ☐ American Express

Card Number: _____

Expiration Date: _____ Security Code: _____

Upon credit card verification, if you are approved for registration as a Bidder, you hereby authorize Julien's Auctions to charge the above listed card for any purchases you make at Auction pursuant to the Auction Terms and Conditions.

Signature: _____ Date: _____

Shipping: Winning Bidders are responsible for all costs to ship their items. Shipping is not included in the Hammer Price of your auction item(s). Some items may be shipped directly by Julien's Auctions, or we may contract with an outside shipping company ("Shippers"), to ship your Lot to you. Please allow 2-12 weeks for the delivery of your Lot; delivery time is dependent upon the size of the Auction, the destination address of the Lot, and the method of transportation to deliver the Lot. Julien's Auctions and Shippers are not responsible for returned or undeliverable shipments. Invoices must be paid in full prior to shipping. Please direct all shipping inquiries to shipping@juliensauctions.com. If you are picking up your items, you will have 30 days to do so. After 30 days, we charge $8.00 per lot, per day, unless prior arrangements are made. The buyer is responsible for all fees including duties, taxes, VAT, Customs, and other unforeseen shipping related charges.

Buyer's Premium: I hereby request approval for registration to bid in this auction sale with Julien's Auctions (the Auctioneer). I acknowledge that I have read, understood and agreed to the Terms and Conditions of the sale as posted on http://www.juliensauctions.com and http://www.julienslive.com, as well as printed in the auction catalogue, applicable to the auction sale for which I now register and request the Auctioneer to approve such registration as an authorized participant as a Floor Bidder (Bidder at live event), Absentee Bidder (Bidder by phone or proxy) or Online Bidder. A buyer's premium will be added to the successful bid price and is payable by the purchaser as part of the total purchase price. I acknowledge and agree that Buyer's Premium will be added to the hammer price on each individual lot as follows:

Lots with a Hammer Price of up to $100.00: Twenty-five United States Dollars and zero cents ($25.00)

Lots with a Hammer Price of $100.01 up to and including $200,000.00: Twenty-five percent (25%)

Lots with a Hammer Price of $200,000.01 and above: Twenty-five percent (25%) will be added to the Hammer Price up to $200,000.00, and an additional Buyer's Premium of twenty percent (20%) will be added to any amount above $200,000.00.

I further acknowledge that I am responsible to pay Julien's Auctions the aggregate of the hammer price and the Buyer's Premium for such lot(s). All invoices must be paid within 10 calendar days after the close of the auction. I authorize Julien's Auctions to charge my credit card listed on this form for all items purchased (including shipping) at this auction, and any future Julien's Auctions I may participate in, if not otherwise paid in full within 10 calendar days after the close of the auction.

Representations And Acknowledgement: I, the undersigned, represent and warrant that the information I have provided on this Bidder Registration Form is truthful, complete, and accurate. I acknowledge receiving a copy of the Auction Terms and Conditions attached hereto, and agree to comply with all provisions therein. I understand that each and every Bid that I place in the Auction creates a binding obligation to purchase the Lots for which I am the winning bidder, and that all purchases are subject to additional fees as detailed in the Auction Terms and Conditions.

Signature: _____ Date: _____

Print Name: _____

Company (if applicable): _____ Title: _____

Please fax completed forms to (310) 388-0207

Forms must be received by 12:00 p.m. (Noon) Pacific Standard Time on the day prior to the auction day in order for your registration information to be timely reviewed and verified.

MAIL ONLY: Julien's Auctions | 8630 Hayden Place | Culver City, CA 90232
phone: (310) 836-1818 | fax: (310) 388-0207 | email: info@juliensauctions.com

Auction Terms and Conditions

Julien Entertainment.com, Inc., a California corporation d/b/a Julien's Auctions ("Julien's Auctions", "Company", "we", "our", or "us") hereby provides the following terms ("Auction Terms and Conditions") to apply to sales by Bids conducted by Julien's Auctions (each an "Auction" and collectively, the "Auctions"). By completing a Bidder Registration Form, you agree that you have read, understood and agree to be bound by these Auction Terms and Conditions.

PLEASE READ THESE AUCTION TERMS AND CONDITIONS CAREFULLY. THESE AUCTION TERMS AND CONDITIONS INCLUDE AN AGREEMENT TO MANDATORY ARBITRATION, WHICH MEANS THAT YOU AGREE TO SUBMIT ANY DISPUTE ARISING UNDER, RELATED TO, OR IN CONNECTION WITH THE AUCTION TO BINDING INDIVIDUAL ARBITRATION RATHER THAN PROCEED IN COURT. THE DISPUTES/ARBITRATION PROVISION ALSO INCLUDES A CLASS ACTION WAIVER, WHICH MEANS THAT YOU AGREE TO PROCEED WITH ANY DISPUTE INDIVIDUALLY AND NOT AS PART OF A CLASS ACTION. THIS AGREEMENT ALSO INCLUDES A JURY WAIVER.

1. AUCTIONS.

Each Auction conducted is of a designated set of items (each a "Lot") on a designated date. Lots are provided by the party that wishes us to sell property on their behalf (each such party a "Consignor"). We will provide the pertinent information for each Auction, including: date, start time of auction, each Lot to be sold, and location. Auctions may be conducted live in-person, online via http://www.julienslive.com (the "Service"), or both. All Auctions conducted by Julien's Auctions, and these Auction Terms and Conditions, are governed by the laws of the State of California. Julien's Auctions maintains a bond on file with the California Secretary of State as required by California Civil Code §1812.600.

2. REGISTRATION.

In order to participate in an Auction, registration is required for all persons wishing to Bid ("Bidders"). Any person registering to Bid by phone, absentee, or in person will complete a Bidder Registration Form. Online Bidders will submit a completed electronic form through the Service, where they may also establish an online account ("Member Account"). Each Auction requires a separate registration; Bidders with a Member Account may register for Auctions via their account.

(a) **Information Required.** To register, Bidders are required to submit their name, physical address, telephone number, email address, and credit card information. You hereby represent that all information you submit in connection with registration is truthful and accurate. By submitting your information, you consent to have your personal information processed by Julien's Auctions in the United States. Julien's Auctions has implemented commercially reasonable technical and organizational measures designed to secure your personal information from accidental loss and from unauthorized access, access, use, alteration or disclosure. However, we cannot guarantee that unauthorized third parties will never be able to defeat those measures or use your personal information for improper purposes. You acknowledge that you provide your personal information at your own risk.

(b) **First Time Bidders.** For verification purposes, Bidders who have not participated in an Auction are required to submit a copy of their (A) official government-issued identification (driver's license /

passport / state identification card), and (B) credit card. Copies of such documents may be submitted in person, via facsimile to 310-388-0207 or via email to **bidding@juliensauctions.com.** Failure to do so may inhibit your ability to register.

(c) **Credit Card Authorization.** We (and/or our third-party payment processor) may verify credit card information in order to register. To verify your card, we will charge $0.01 to it. After the card is verified, we will immediately refund the card. Your card issuer will credit your card balance within thirty (30) days from the date of the refund. In the event you add or replace a credit card, we may also verify such new or replacement credit card.

(d) **Minors.** Bids will not be accepted from those persons under eighteen (18) years of age (i) without written consent of said person's parent or legal guardian, or (ii) unless such person is an emancipated minor. Written consent must acknowledge the terms and conditions of sale. This written consent constitutes an agreement to be bound thereby on behalf of the Bidder. If you are under 18 years of age you may participate in Auctions only if you are either an emancipated minor, or possess legal parental or guardian consent, and are fully able and competent to enter into the terms, conditions, obligations, affirmations, representations, and warranties set forth in these Auction Terms and Conditions, and to abide by and comply with these Auction Terms and Conditions.

IF YOU ARE A PARENT OR GUARDIAN AND YOU PROVIDE YOUR CONSENT TO THE REGISTRATION OF YOUR CHILD, YOU AGREE TO BE BOUND BY THIS AGREEMENT WITH RESPECT TO, THROUGH, AND IN CONNECTION WITH SUCH REGISTRATION AND AUCTION PARTICIPATION.

(e) **Online Member Accounts.** Bidder can elect to set up a Member Account on the Service in accordance with the policies set forth on the Service. Bidder acknowledges and agrees that all Bids placed under a Member Account are considered to be placed by the Member or with Member's authorization.

(f) **Approval of Registration.** Julien's Auctions, in its sole and absolute discretion, reserves the right to approve or reject Bidders for its Auctions at any time. We are under no obligation to accept your application for registration.

(g) **Term of Registration.** Upon approval by Julien's Auctions, your registration is effective throughout the applicable Auction for which you registered and any post-Auction obligations you incur in connection with Bids you placed during such Auction.

3. BIDDING.

Upon completed and approved registration, Bidders may submit a binding offer to purchase a Lot at a specified price (a "Bid") in an Auction.

(a) **Placement; Payment Authorization.** When a Lot at the Auction goes live, you are free to place bids on such Lot (i) if an in-person Auction, or if an Auction conducted both in-person and online, until the individual conducting the sale for Julien's Auctions (the "Auctioneer") determines that bidding on such Lot has closed, or (ii) if an online-only Auction, in accordance with the parameters set forth on the Service for such Lot. As bids are placed, Julien's Auctions reserves the right to authorize your credit card for any bid amount placed. If an authorization was made on a Bid and you

are subsequently outbid, Julien's Auctions will release that authorization.

(b) **Notifications.** If you are placing Bids via the Service or by proxy, each time you are outbid Julien's Auctions will send you an email message notification advising you of such. If you are a telephone or in-person Bidder, it is your responsibility to monitor the Lot(s) for which you placed Bid(s) in the event you are outbid. If you are the Winning Bidder for a given Lot, Julien's Auctions will send you an email message confirmation.

(c) **Bid Conditions.** Julien's Auctions reserves the right to accept or decline any Bid. Bids must be for an entire Lot. Each Lot constitutes a separate sale. All Bids are per Lot unless otherwise announced at a live sale by the Auctioneer. All winning Bids are subject to a Buyer's Premium (as defined herein). Live auction Lots will be sold in their numbered sequence unless the Auctioneer directs otherwise. Julien's Auctions may cancel any Lot and have it removed from an Auction prior to acceptance of a winning Bid. In the event a Lot is removed from an Auction, notice will be provided (i) if an online Auction, by a posting on the Service and by email to Bidders who placed their Bid on such Lot via the Service, and (ii) if the Auction is an in-person Auction, at the physical location of the Auction. In such instance of Lot removal from an Auction, any Bids previously placed on such Lot prior to its removal from the Auction shall be cancelled, and Julien's Auctions will not receive any further Bids on such Lot.

(d) **Purchase Obligations.** In connection with making Bids, Bidders agree that the registered Bidder with the highest Bid at the close of the Auction will be obligated to purchase the Lot. By bidding on any Lot, you agree to purchase the Lot at the price you have Bid. You agree that should you Bid on a Lot and that Bid is the winning Bid, that you are bound to pay Julien's Auctions the winning bid amount for the Lot. You further acknowledge and agree that the winning Bid you submit for each Lot is subject to: (i) additional fees, including the Buyer's Premium and Online Service Fee (if applicable), and (ii) additional costs, including taxes, shipping (if applicable), storage (if applicable), and customs (if applicable), and that you are obligated to pay such fees and costs in connection with your winning Bid.

(e) **Conduct.** It is unlawful and illegal for Bidders to collude, pool, or agree with another Bidder to pay less than the fair value for Lot(s). Bidders participating in both live and online auctions acknowledge that the law provides for substantial penalties for those who violate these provisions.

(f) **Disputes Between Bidders.** For live auctions the Auctioneer will have final discretion in the event that any dispute should arise between Bidders. The Auctioneer will determine the successful Bidder, cancel the sale, or re-offer and resell the Lot or Lots in dispute. Julien's Auctions will have final discretion to resolve any disputes arising after the sale and in online auctions. If any dispute arises our sale record is conclusive.

(g) **Absentee Bids.** Julien's Auctions will execute order or absentee bids, and accept telephone bids as a courtesy to clients who are unable to attend the live auctions. Notwithstanding the foregoing, we take no responsibility for any errors or omissions in connection with this courtesy.

(h) **Online Bids.** Our online auction Service is provided "As Is" and "As Available." High speed internet access is required to access the Service effectively. The Service is subject to limitations, delays and other problems inherent in the use of the Internet and electronic communications. Julien's Auctions is not responsible for any delays, delivery failures, or other damage resulting from such problems.

(i) **Reserve**. All of the Lots offered at Auction are subject to a confidential minimum price acceptable to the Consignor at which the Lot will be sold (the "Reserve"). Julien's Auctions is not obligated to sell the Lot unless the Reserve is met. A Lot or Lots may be withdrawn from an Auction if there is no Bid equal to or above the Reserve.

During a live auction the Auctioneer may open any Lot by bidding on behalf of the Consignor and may bid up to the amount of the Reserve, by placing successive or consecutive bids for a Lot or Bids in response to other Bidders. Online sales may do the same by employing the use of a starting Bid which will commence bidding at or below the reserve price agreed to by the Consignor.

4. WINNING BIDS.

At the close of the Auction, the highest Bid for a Lot will be considered the "Hammer Price", and the successful Bidder shall be informed by email (the "Winning Bidder" or the "Purchaser"). The Winning Bidder is responsible for paying to Julien's Auctions the Hammer Price, Buyer's Premium, and all applicable taxes, plus shipping costs (if applicable), insurance costs while in transit (for items not picked up in person), Online Service Fee (if the Winning Bidder placed the Bid online via the Service) and any applicable customs and/or duties (such amounts collectively, the "Total Purchase Price"). Upon conclusion of the Auction, we will provide the Winning Bidder with an accounting statement of the Total Purchase Price by email.

(a) **Risk of Loss; Release of Lots**. Upon establishment of the Hammer Price for the purchase of the Lot (the "Sale"), the Winning Bidder immediately thereafter assumes full responsibility for all risk of loss or damage (including, without limitation, liability for or damage to frames or glass covering prints, paintings, photos, or other works) and will immediately pay the Total Purchase Price or such part as Julien's Auctions may require. All Sales are final. Lots will be released to you (or the shipping company, as applicable) upon our receipt of payment of the Total Purchase Price in full from you.

(b) **Buyer's Premium**. Winning Bidder agrees that in addition to the Hammer Price, the Lot will be subject to an additional charge on the Hammer Price as part of the total purchase price (the "Buyer's Premium"). The Buyer's Premium is as follows:

Lots with a Hammer Price of up to $100.00. For individual Lots with a Hammer Price of up to and including one hundred United States Dollars and zero cents ($100.00), the Buyer's Premium is twenty-five United States Dollars and zero cents ($25.00).

Lots with a Hammer Price of $100.01 up to and including $200,000.00. For individual Lots with a Hammer Price of one hundred United States Dollars and one cent ($100.01) to two hundred thousand United States Dollars and zero cents ($200,000.00), a Buyer's Premium of twenty-five percent (25%) will be added to the Hammer Price.

Example: The Hammer Price on a Lot is one hundred and fifty thousand United States Dollars ($150,000). The Winning Bidder would pay a Buyer's Premium of 25%, i.e., thirty-seven thousand five hundred United States Dollars ($37,500.00) on such Lot.

Lots with a Hammer Price of $200,000.01 and above. For individual Lots with a Hammer Price of two hundred thousand United States Dollars and one cent ($200,000.01) and above, a Buyer's Premium of twenty-five percent (25%) will be added to the Hammer Price up to $200,000.00, and an additional Buyer's Premium of twenty percent (20%) will be added to any amount above $200,000.00.

Example: The Hammer Price on a Lot is two hundred and fifty thousand United States Dollars ($250,000.00). The Winning Bidder would pay a total Buyer's Premium of sixty thousand United States Dollars ($60,000.00) on such Lot, calculated as follows: 25% of the first $200,000.00, i.e. fifty thousand United States Dollars ($50,000.00), plus 20% of the remaining $50,000.00, i.e. ten thousand United States Dollars.

(c) **Online Service Fee**. For all Lots where the Winning Bid is submitted online via the Service, an additional three percent (3%) of the Hammer Price (the "Online Service Fee") will be added to the Buyer's Premium amount detailed immediately above.

Example: The Hammer Price on a Lot is two hundred and fifty thousand United States Dollars ($250,000.00), with the highest Bid being placed online via the Service. The Winning Bidder would pay, in addition to the Buyer's Premium, an Online Service Fee of seven thousand five hundred United States Dollars ($7,500.00).

(d) **Taxes**. Winning Bidder agrees that he/she is responsible for the payment of any and all applicable taxes due in connection with such Lot, including but not limited to sales tax, use tax, and value-added tax (VAT). All items picked up in California will be charged California state sales tax, as will all items sent to California residents. All items sent to New York residents will be charged New York state sales tax.

(e) **Lot Retrieval**. All Lots must be removed from our premises by the Winning Bidder within thirty (30) calendar days of the conclusion of the Auction at the Winning Bidder's own expense.

In-person Pick-up; Storage Fees. If you intend to pick up your items as the Winning Bidder, arrangements must be made upon your notice to us in conjunction with payment of the Total Purchase Price for the Lot. If, after thirty (30) days following your payment of the Total Purchase Price, the Lot is not removed: (A) a handling charge of eight dollars ($8.00) per day or one percent (1%) of the Total Purchase Price per month, whichever is greater, will be payable to us by the Winning Bidder, with a minimum of five hundred dollars ($500.00) or five percent (5%) of the Total Purchase Price for any Lot not so removed within sixty (60) calendar days after the Sale, whichever is greater (the "Storage Fees"); and (B) we may send the Lot to a public warehouse or storage facility, at Winning Bidder's sole risk and expense. If Winning Bidder fails to remove the Lot within one hundred and eighty (180) days following the Sale, then, in addition to the Storage Fees, Julien's Auctions shall have the right (but not the obligation) to dispose of or retain any such Lot. All costs incurred by Julien's Auctions in connection with the removal or disposal of any such Lot shall be paid by Winning Bidder within ten (10) days of our demand therefor.

Shipping. Winning Bidders are responsible for all costs to ship their items. Shipping is not included in the Hammer Price of your auction items. Please review the shipping terms for your items. Some items may be shipped directly by Julien's Auctions, or we may contract with an outside shipping company ("Shippers"), to ship your Lot to you. Please allow 2-12 weeks for the delivery of your Lot to you; delivery time is dependent

upon the size of the Auction, the destination address of the Lot, and the method of transportation to deliver the Lot. Julien's Auctions and Shippers are not responsible for returned or undeliverable shipments.

International. Julien's Auctions will provide you with a customs document detailing the value of items purchased. Julien's Auctions and Shippers are not responsible if there are any delays in customs. Purchasers are responsible for compliance with all laws and regulations applicable to the international purchase and shipment of items. Purchaser understands that the shipment of Lots internationally is subject to United States export controls and trade and economic sanctions laws, and agrees to comply with all such laws and regulations, including the Export Administration Regulations maintained by the United States Department of Commerce, and the trade and economic sanctions maintained by the United States Treasury Department's Office of Foreign Assets Control.

(f) **Invoices and Payments**. All invoices must be paid within ten (10) calendar days after the close of the Auction.

Payments. Julien's Auctions accepts payment by cashier's check, personal check, wire transfer, American Express, MasterCard, and Visa. Winning Bidders who wish to pay by check may do so by making checks payable to: Julien's Auctions, 8630 Hayden Place, Culver City, CA 90232.

Credit Card Authorization. Bidder authorizes Julien's Auctions to charge Bidder's credit card provided at registration for all items purchased at any Auction that Bidder may participate in, if not paid in full within ten (10) calendar days after the close of the Auction. Processing fees for credit card payments may apply. All invoices under five thousand United States Dollars ($5,000.00) will automatically be charged to the credit card on file unless prior arrangements are made.

Lot Rights. In the event Julien's Auctions has agreed in writing prior to the auction to provide payment terms or an extended period of time for payment to you, you acknowledge and agree that you shall have no right, title, or interest in and to any property purchased by you until all amounts owed by you are paid in full.

If you fail to comply with the terms of the payment plan or extended payment period, upon your default, Julien's Auctions shall have the unequivocal right, at its sole discretion, to sell some or all of the property on which you were the Winning Bidder, and to apply the proceeds toward the balance of any monies owed by you to Julien's Auctions. If the monies received through the sale of the items do not meet your outstanding obligations, Julien's Auctions shall have the right to pursue any and all remedies available under the law against you pursuant to the provisions set forth herein. If the monies received through the sale of the items exceed your outstanding obligations, the excess, minus any fees or costs incurred by Julien's Auctions in connection with and arising out of the sale of the properties, shall be refunded to you.

Late Payment Fees. Commencing with the tenth day following the Sale, payments not received by Julien's Auctions will incur a late charge of one-and-a-half percent (1.5%) per month (or the highest rate allowable by law, whichever is lower) on the outstanding Total Purchase Price.

Excess Fund Return. In the event you are the Winning Bidder on a Lot and prior to an Auction you provided us with a deposit for your Bid which exceeds the Total Purchase Price, we will return any such excess within thirty

(30) business days of the conclusion of the Auction, unless delay is compelled by (A) legal proceedings, or (B) our inability, through no fault of our own, to transfer title to the Lot or comply with any provision of California Civil Code Section 1812.600-1812.609, the California Commercial Code, the California Code of Civil Procedure, or other provision of applicable law.

(g) **Defaults; Company's Remedies**. If Winning Bidder does not comply with the conditions herein, such Winning Bidder will be in default. In addition to any and all other remedies available to Julien's Auctions and the Consignor by law and at equity, including, without limitation, the right to hold the Winning Bidder liable for the Total Purchase Price, including all fees, charges and expenses more fully set forth herein, we, at our option, may: (a) cancel the Sale of the subject Lot, or any other lots sold to the defaulting Purchaser at the same or any other Auction, retaining as liquidated damages all payments made by the Purchaser; (b) resell the purchased property, whether at public auction or by private sale; or (c) effect any combination thereof. In any case, the Purchaser will be liable for any deficiency, any and all costs, handling charges, late charges, expenses of both sales, our commissions on both sales at our regular rates, legal fees and expenses, collection fees and incidental damages.

We may, in our sole discretion, apply any proceeds of sale then due or thereafter becoming due to the Purchaser from us or any affiliated company, or any payment made by the Purchaser to us or any affiliated company, where or not intended to reduce the Purchaser's obligations with respect to the unpaid Lot or Lots, to the deficiency and any other amounts due to us or any affiliated companies. In addition, a defaulting Purchaser will be deemed to have granted and assigned to us and our affiliated companies, a continuing security interest of first priority in any property or money of our owing to such Purchaser in our possession or in the possession of any of our affiliated companies, and we may retain and apply such property or money as collateral security for the obligations due to us or to any affiliated company of ours. Payment will not be deemed to have been made in full until we have collected good funds. In the event the purchaser fails to pay any or all of the Total Purchase Price for any Lot and Julien's Auctions elects to pay the Consignor any portion of the sale proceeds, the purchaser acknowledges that Julien's Auctions shall have all of the rights of the Consignor to pursue the Purchaser for any amounts paid to the Consignor, whether at law, in equity, or under these Auction Terms and Conditions.

Julien's Auctions further reserves the right to prohibit defaulting Purchasers from being approved for registration at future Auctions.

5. LIMITATION OF LIABILITY.

(a) **Exclusion of Consequential Damages**. TO THE MAXIMUM EXTENT PERMITTED BY APPLICABLE LAW, IN NO EVENT SHALL JULIEN'S AUCTIONS, ITS AFFIL-IATES, OFFICERS, DIRECTORS, EMPLOYEES, AGENTS, OR ITS LICENSORS BE LIABLE FOR ANY DIRECT, INDIRECT, PUNITIVE, INCIDENTAL, SPECIAL, CONSEQUENTIAL OR EXEMPLARY DAMAGES, INCLUDING WITHOUT LIMITATION DAMAGES FOR LOSS OF PROFITS, GOODWILL, USE, DATA OR OTHER INTANGIBLE LOSSES, ARISING OUT OF OR RELATING TO THESE AUCTION TERMS AND CONDI-TIONS, REGARDLESS OF THE THEORY OF LIABILITY, EVEN IF ADVISED OF THE POSSIBILITY OF SUCH DAMAGES. THROUGHOUT THE AUCTION, JULIEN'S AUCTIONS IS NOT RESPONSIBLE FOR THE CON-DUCT (WHETHER ONLINE OR OFFLINE) OF ANY BIDDER, CONSIGNOR, OR NON-COMPANY PERSON-NEL.

(b) **Liability Cap**. COMPANY'S MAXIMUM AGGREGATE LIABILITY ARISING OUT OF OR RELATING TO THIS AGREEMENT, REGARDLESS OF THE THEORY OF LIABILITY, WILL BE LIMITED TO THE GREATER OF FIVE HUNDRED DOLLARS ($500) AND THE TOTAL PURCHASE PRICE PAID OR PAYABLE BY YOU TO JULIEN'S AUCTIONS. THE EXISTENCE OF MORE THAN ONE CLAIM SHALL NOT EXPAND SUCH LIMIT. THE PARTIES ACKNOWLEDGE THAT THE FEES AGREED UPON BETWEEN YOU AND JULIEN'S AUC-TIONS ARE BASED IN PART ON THESE LIMITATIONS, AND THAT THESE LIMITATIONS WILL APPLY NOTWITHSTANDING ANY FAILURE OF ANY ESSEN-TIAL PURPOSE OF ANY LIMITED REMEDY. THE FOREGOING LIMITATION OF LIABILITY SHALL APPLY TO THE FULLEST EXTENT PERMITTED BY LAW IN THE APPLICABLE JURISDICTION.

6. INDEMNITY.

You agree to defend, indemnify and hold harmless Julien's Auctions and its subsidiaries, agents, and other affiliated companies, and the employees, contractors, agents, officers and directors of each, from and against any and all claims, damages, obligations, losses, liabili-ties, costs or debt, and expenses (including but not limited to attorney's fees) arising from your violation of any term of these Auction Terms and Conditions, includ-ing without limitation, (i) your breach of any of the representations and warranties herein; (ii) your violation of any law, rule or regulation of the United States or any other country.

7. LOTS.

(a) **Warranty; Disclaimers**. Julien's Auctions warrants the authenticity of Attribution (as defined below) of property listed in the catalogue or online as stated in the Attribution Warranty in Section 8 below. Except for the Attribution Warranty, all property is sold "As Is". We make no warranties, nor does the Consignor, as to the merchantability or fitness for a particular purpose, the correctness of the catalogue or other description of the physical condition, size, quality, rarity, importance, medium, provenance, exhibitions, literature or historical relevance of any property. No oral or written statements made in the catalogue, online listing, advertisement, Condition Report, bill of sale, and announcement or elsewhere made by employees (including affiliated and related companies) shall be considered a warranty. We and the Consignor make no representations and warranties, express or implied, as to whether the purchaser acquires any Intellectual Property Rights, including but not limited to, any reproduction rights of any property. We and the Consignor are not responsible for errors and omissions in the catalogue, online listings or any other supplemental material.

(b) **Evaluation; Item Descriptions**. It is the sole responsibility and risk of prospective Bidders to make the determination of whether a Lot is suitable for Bid.

(c) **Catalogues**. While Julien's Auctions customarily produces printed catalogues of all Lots available for an Auction, such catalogues are for illustrative purposes only. Descriptions of Lots therein are not comprehensive and may contain errors. We do not warrant any aspect of content in our catalogues other than the Attribution of Lots.

(d) **Condition Reports**. Bidders may request a written report of the Lot's repair and restoration history (a "Condition Report") by emailing info@juliensauctions.com for a Condition Report. Other than Attribution, we do not make any representations or warranties, express or implied, concerning any content in a Condition Report. We will customarily provide Condition Reports so long as we receive a written request from you at least forty-eight (48) hours prior to the Auction. You agree that any Condition Report(s) we provide to you are the confidential information of Julien's Auctions, are to be utilized for your personal purposes only, are to be treated by you with the same degree of care that you utilize to protect your own confidential information (provided, however, that you must at least use reasonable care), and are not to be disclosed to third parties unless mandated by law. If you breach any obligations in this Section, Julien's Auctions shall be entitled to seek equitable relief to protect its interest therein, including but not limited to injunctive relief as well as money damages. These confidentiality obligations will survive the conclusion of any Auction.

(e) **Pricing**. All Lot pricing is listed in United States Dollars. We may offer certain programs, tools, and site experiences of particular interest to international users, such as estimated local currency conversion and inter-national shipping calculation tools, but these are offered for convenience only.

8. ATTRIBUTION WARRANTY.

(a) **Attribution**. "Attribution" is defined by Julien's Auctions as the creator, period, culture, or source of origin, as the case may be as stated in the (i) Heading set forth in bold type of a Lot in a live auction catalogue, as amended by any statements by the Auctioneer and/or written salesroom notices and announcements ("Bold Type Heading") or (ii) the lot Title of an online auction, as amended by any online notices and announcements ("Online Lot Heading") (Bold Type Heading and Online Lot Heading collectively, "Headings").

(b) **Attribution Warranty**. Subject to the exclusions below, we make no warranties to information not contained in Headings. Subject to the exclusions listed below, Julien's Auctions warrants the Attribution of a Lot for a period of one (1) year from the date of Sale and only to the original Purchaser on record at the auction. If it is determined to our satisfaction that the Attribution is incorrect, the Sale will be rescinded if the Lot is returned to the Julien's Auctions warehouse facility in the same condition in which it was at the time of Sale. In order to satisfy us that the "Attribution" of a lot is indeed incorrect we reserve the right to require the Purchaser to obtain, at the Purchaser's expense, the opinion of two experts in the field, mutually acceptable to Julien's Auctions and the Purchaser, before we agree to rescind the Sale under the warranty. This warranty is not assignable and applies only to the original Purchaser on record with Julien's Auctions. This warranty does not transfer to any subsequent owners of any purchased property (this includes without limitation, heirs, successors, beneficiaries or assigns).

(c) **Remedies**. Should a Sale be rescinded and the Total Purchase Price paid, it is specifically understood that this will be considered the sole remedy. It is exclusive and in lieu of any other remedy available as a matter of law, or in equity.

(d) **Exclusions**. Exclusions will be made and this warranty does not apply to Attribution which on the date of sale was in accordance with the then generally accepted opinion of scholars and specialists, or the identification of periods or dates of execution which may be proven inaccurate by means of scientific processes not generally accepted for use until after publication of the catalogue or listing online, or which were unreasonably expensive or impractical to employ.

9. INTELLECTUAL PROPERTY.

Julien's Auctions retains all right, title, and interest (including, without limitation, all Intellectual Property Rights) in and to the items outlined in this Section, and all derivatives, modifications, or enhancements thereto. You agree to take any action reasonably requested by Julien's Auctions to evidence, maintain, enforce or defend our Intellectual Property Rights. You shall not take any action to jeopardize, encumber, limit or interfere in any manner with Julien's Auctions ownership of and rights with respect to the items outlined in this Section. All rights not expressly licensed to you in these Auction Terms and Conditions are expressly reserved by Julien's Auctions.

(a) **Definition**. "Intellectual Property Right" means any patent, copyright, trade or service mark, trade dress, trade name, database right, goodwill, logo, trade secret right, or any other intellectual property right or proprietary information right, in each case whether registered or unregistered, and whether arising in any jurisdiction, including without limitation all rights of registrations, applications, and renewals thereof and causes of action for infringement or misappropriation related to any of the foregoing.

(b) **Content**. The Auction, the Service, and all materials, including, without limitation, software, images, text, graphics, illustrations, logos, catalogues, Condition Reports, patents, trademarks, service marks, copyrights, photographs, audio, videos and music (the "Content"), and all Intellectual Property Rights related thereto, are the exclusive property of Julien's Auctions and its licensors. Except as explicitly provided herein, nothing in this Agreement shall be deemed to create a license in or under any such Intellectual Property Rights, and you agree not to sell, license, rent, modify, distribute, copy, reproduce, transmit, publicly display, publicly perform, publish, adapt, edit or create derivative works from any materials or Content made available to you by Julien's Auctions orally or in writing regardless of form of media. Use of the Content for any purpose not expressly permitted by these Auction Terms and Conditions is strictly prohibited.

(c) **Trademarks**. "Julien's Auctions", "The Auction House to the Stars", "Julien's Auctions The Auction House to the Stars", and other logos and service names are trademarks, registered trademarks or trade dress of Julien Entertainment.com, Inc. Julien's Auctions trademarks and trade dress may not be used in connection with any product or service that is not ours, in any manner that is likely to cause confusion among customers, or in any manner that disparages or discredits Julien's Auctions.

(d) **Data**. Julien's Auctions owns the aggregate, statistical, and sales data related to, derived from, and concerning its Auctions, and reserves all Intellectual Property Rights to utilize such data for its own business purposes.

(e) **Ideas and Comments**. You may choose to, or we may invite you to, submit comments or ideas about our Auctions, including without limitation about how to improve our operations, our Service, and/or our products ("Ideas"). By submitting any Idea, you agree that your disclosure is gratuitous, unsolicited and without restriction and will not place Julien's Auctions under any fiduciary or other obligation, that we are free to disclose the Ideas on a non-confidential basis to anyone or otherwise use the Ideas without any additional compensation to you. You acknowledge that, by acceptance of your Idea submission, Julien's Auctions does not waive any rights to use similar or related ideas previously known to Julien's Auctions, or developed by its

employees, or obtained from sources other than you.

10. DISPUTES.

PLEASE READ THIS SECTION CAREFULLY. IT INCLUDES A **MANDATORY ARBITRATION PROVISION**, WHICH MEANS THAT YOU AGREE TO SUBMIT ANY DISPUTE RELATED TO YOUR USE OF ANY OF THE SITES TO BINDING INDIVIDUAL ARBITRATION RATHER THAN PROCEED IN COURT. THIS PROVISION ALSO INCLUDES A **CLASS ACTION WAIVER**, WHICH MEANS THAT YOU AGREE TO PROCEED WITH ANY DISPUTE INDIVIDUALLY AND NOT AS PART OF A CLASS ACTION. THIS SECTION ALSO INCLUDES A **JURY WAIVER**.

You and Julien's Auctions agree that any dispute, controversy, or claim that has arisen or may arise between us relating in any way to your use of or access to the Auction, the Service, any interpretation, breach, enforcement, or termination of these Auction Terms and Conditions, or otherwise relating to Julien's Auctions in any way (collectively, "Covered Matters") will be resolved in accordance with the provisions set forth in this Section 10.

(a) **Informal Resolution**. If you have any dispute with us, you agree that before taking any formal action, you will contact us at info@juliensauctions.com, provide a brief, written description of the dispute and your contact information (including your username, if your dispute relates to an account) and allow sixty (60) days to pass, during which we will attempt to reach an amicable resolution of your issue.

(b) **Applicable Law**. The laws of the State of California, and applicable federal law, will govern all Covered Matters. California conflicts of law rules shall apply.

(c) **Arbitration**. **Subject only to the optional exceptions in Paragraph 10(e) below, You and Julien's Auctions each agree that any and all disputes, claims, or controversies that have arisen, or may arise, between you and Julien's Auctions relating in any way to or arising out of this or previous versions of the Auction Terms and Conditions or the breach, termination, enforcement, interpretation or validity thereof, your use of or access to our services, or any products or services sold, offered, or purchased through Company's services shall be resolved exclusively through final and binding arbitration, rather than in court.** Any claims arising out of, relating to, or connected with these Auction Terms and Conditions not resolved through Informal Resolution pursuant to paragraph 10(a) above must be asserted individually in a binding arbitration to be administered by JAMS in Los Angeles County, California pursuant to the JAMS Comprehensive Arbitration Rules and Procedures. Both parties further agree that the arbitration shall be conducted before a single JAMS arbitrator who is a retired California or federal judge or justice. The arbitrator shall strictly apply California substantive law and the California Rules of Evidence. BY AGREEING TO ARBITRATE, YOU WAIVE ANY RIGHT YOU HAVE TO A COURT OR JURY TRIAL. The arbitrator shall not conduct any form of class or collective arbitration nor join or consolidate claims by or for individuals. The arbitrator, and not any federal, state, or local court or agency, shall have exclusive authority to resolve any dispute relating to the interpretation, applicability, enforceability or formation of these Auction Terms and Conditions, including, any claim that all or any part of these Auction Terms and Conditions is void or voidable or that a particular claim is subject to arbitration. Judgment on the award rendered by the arbitrator may be entered in any court of competent jurisdiction.

(d) **Award**. You agree and acknowledge that in any award to be granted by the Arbitrator, your rights and remedies against us or any distributor of financier or other party related to the Auction or Service shall be limited to an action at law for money damages, and you hereby waive all other rights and remedies you may have at law or in equity (including, without limitation, injunctive relief, rescission, cancellation, and termination of this Agreement or the right to enjoin or restrain the advertisement, promotion, marketing or exploitation by Julien's Auctions or any third party in connection with the Auction and/or any rights or activities hereunder in any and all manner of media whatsoever, whether now known or hereafter devised). For matters where the relief sought is over $5,000, the arbitrator's decision will include the essential findings and conclusions upon which the arbitrator based the award. The arbitrator will decide the substance of all claims in accordance with applicable law, including recognized principles of equity, and will honor all claims of privilege recognized by law. The arbitrator's award of damages must be consistent with the terms of the "Limitation of Liability" section as to the types and the amounts of damages for which a party may be held liable. The arbitrator shall not be bound by rulings in prior arbitrations involving different users, but is bound by rulings in prior arbitrations involving the same Julien's Auctions user to the extent required by applicable law. The arbitrator's award shall be final and binding and judgment on the award rendered by the arbitrator may be entered in any court having jurisdiction thereof. THE ARBITRATOR MAY AWARD RELIEF (INCLUDING MONETARY, INJUNCTIVE, AND DECLARATORY RELIEF) ONLY IN FAVOR OF THE INDIVIDUAL PARTY SEEKING RELIEF AND ONLY TO THE EXTENT NECESSARY TO PROVIDE RELIEF NECESSITATED BY THAT PARTY'S INDIVIDUAL CLAIM(S). ANY RELIEF AWARDED CANNOT AFFECT OTHER USERS.

(e) **Exceptions**. There are only two exceptions in which the parties may elect to seek resolution outside of Arbitration before JAMS:

(i) First, if we reasonably believe that you have in any manner infringed upon or violated or threatened to violate or infringe any of our Intellectual Property Rights, privacy rights, publicity rights, or data security, in which case you acknowledge that there may be no adequate remedy at law and we may seek injunctive or other appropriate relief in any court of competent jurisdiction, without any attempt at informal resolution pursuant to paragraph 10(a) above.

(ii) Second, any claim of $500 or less may, at the option of the claiming party, be resolved in small claims court in Los Angeles County, California, if the claim and the parties are within the jurisdiction of the small claims court and so long as the matter remains in such court and advances only on an individual (non-class, non-representative) basis.

(f) **Costs of Arbitration**. Payment of all filing, administration, and arbitrator fees will be governed by JAMS rules, unless otherwise stated in this agreement to arbitrate. If the value of the relief sought is $5,000 or less, at your request, Julien's Auctions will reimburse you for all filing, administration, and arbitrator fees associated with the arbitration following the earlier of the arbitrator's decision or settlement. In the event the arbitrator determines the claim(s) you assert in the arbitration to be frivolous, Julien's Auctions is relieved of its obligation to reimburse you for any fees associated with the arbitration. The prevailing party shall be entitled to an award of all attorneys' fees, costs and expenses incurred by it in connection with the dispute. "Attorneys' fees and expenses" includes, without limitation, paralegals' fees and expenses, attorneys' consultants' fees and expenses, expert witness' fees and expenses, and all other expenses incurred by the prevailing party or its attorneys in the course of their representation of the prevailing party in anticipation of and/or during the course of the litigation, whether or not otherwise recoverable as "attorneys' fees" or as "costs" under California law; and the same may be sought and awarded in accordance with California procedure as pertaining to an award of contractual attorneys' fees.

(g) **Future Amendments to the Agreement to Arbitrate**. Notwithstanding any provision in the Auction Terms and Conditions to the contrary, you and we agree that if we make any amendment to this agreement to arbitrate in the future, that amendment shall not apply to any claim that was filed in a legal proceeding against Julien's Auctions prior to the effective date of the amendment. The amendment shall apply to all other disputes or claims governed by the agreement to arbitrate that have arisen or may arise between you and Julien's Auctions. If you do not agree to these amended terms, you may close your account within thirty (30) days of the posting or notification and you will not be bound by the amended terms.

(h) **Judicial Forum for Legal Disputes**. Unless you and we agree otherwise, in the event that the agreement to arbitrate above is found not to apply to you or to a particular claim or dispute, either as a result of your decision to opt out of the agreement to arbitrate, as a result of a decision by the arbitrator or a court order or because of an election pursuant to Paragraph 10(e) above, you agree that any claim, controversy, or dispute that has arisen or may arise between you and Julien's Auctions must be resolved exclusively by a state, federal, or small claims court located in Los Angeles County, California. You and Julien's Auctions agree to submit to the exclusive personal jurisdiction of the courts located within Los Angeles County, California for the purpose of litigating all such claims or disputes.

(i) **Opt-Out**. IF YOU ARE A NEW JULIEN'S AUCTIONS USER, YOU CAN CHOOSE TO REJECT THE AGREEMENT TO ARBITRATE PROVISION ("OPT-OUT") BY EMAILING US AN OPT-OUT NOTICE TO ARBITRATIONOPTOUT@JULIENSAUCTIONS.COM ("OPT-OUT NOTICE") OR VIA US MAIL TO: Julien Entertainment.com, Inc., 8630 Hayden Place, Culver City, CA 90232. THE OPT-OUT NOTICE MUST BE RECEIVED NO LATER THAN THIRTY (30) DAYS AFTER THE DATE YOU ACCEPT THESE TERMS FOR THE FIRST TIME. IF YOU ARE NOT A NEW JULIEN'S AUCTIONS USER, YOU HAVE UNTIL THIRTY (30) DAYS AFTER THE POSTING OF THE NEW TERMS TO SUBMIT AN ARBITRATION OPT-OUT NOTICE.

(j) **Procedure**. In order to opt-out, you must email your name, complete address (including street address, city, state, and zip code), and email address(es) associated with your Member account(s) to which the opt-out applies and an unaltered digital image of a valid driver's license or valid government issued photo ID which matches the name on your account to: arbitrationoptout@juliensauctions.com. This procedure is the only way you can opt out of the agreement to arbitrate. If you opt out of the agreement to arbitrate, all other parts of these Auction Terms and Conditions and its Disputes Section will continue to apply to you. Opting out of this agreement to arbitrate has no effect on any previous, other, or future arbitration agreements that you may have with us.

(k) **WAIVER**. BY AGREEING TO THESE AUCTION TERMS AND CONDITIONS, YOU HEREBY IRREVOCABLY WAIVE ANY RIGHT YOU MAY HAVE TO A COURT TRIAL (OTHER THAN SMALL CLAIMS COURT AS PROVIDED ABOVE), A JURY TRIAL, OR TO SERVE AS A REPRESENTATIVE, AS A PRIVATE ATTORNEY GENERAL, OR IN ANY OTHER REPRESENTATIVE CAPACITY, OR TO PARTICIPATE AS A MEMBER OF A CLASS OF CLAIMANTS, IN ANY LAWSUIT, ARBITRATION OR OTHER PROCEEDING FILED AGAINST US AND/OR RELATED THIRD PARTIES.

(l) **STATUTE OF LIMITATIONS AND WAIVER OF CLAIMS**. REGARDLESS OF ANY STATUTE OR LAW TO THE CONTRARY, ANY CLAIM OR CAUSE OF ACTION ARISING OUT OF OR RELATED TO USE OF THE SITE, SERVICE, OR THIS AGREEMENT MUST BE FILED WITHIN ONE (1) YEAR AFTER SUCH CLAIM OR CAUSE OF ACTION ARISES OR IT WILL BE FOREVER WAIVED AND BARRED.

11. MISCELLANEOUS PROVISIONS.

(a) **Governing Law**. These Auction Terms and Conditions will be governed by and construed in accordance with the laws of the State of California and the applicable federal laws of the United States of America. California conflicts of law rules shall apply.

(b) **Force Majeure**. Except for the obligation to pay money, neither party will be liable for any failure or delay in its performance under these Auction Terms and Conditions due to any cause beyond its reasonable control, including acts of war, acts of God, earthquake, flood, weather conditions, embargo, riot, epidemic, acts of terrorism, acts or omissions of vendors or suppliers, equipment failures, sabotage, labor shortage or dispute, governmental act, failure of the Internet or other acts beyond such party's reasonable control, provided that the delayed party: (i) gives the other party prompt notice of such cause; and (ii) uses reasonable commercial efforts to correct promptly such failure or delay in performance.

(c) **Counterparts; Facsimile**. These Auction Terms and Conditions may be executed in any number of counterparts and in facsimile or electronically, each of which shall be an original but all of which together shall constitute one and the same instrument.

(d) **Entire Agreement**. These Auction Terms and Conditions contains the entire understanding of the parties in respect of its subject matter and supersedes all prior agreements and understandings (oral or written) between the parties with respect to such subject matter.

(e) **Modifications**. Any modification, amendment, or addendum to these Auction Terms and Conditions must be in writing and signed by both parties.

(f) **Assignment**. You may not assign these Auction Terms and Conditions or any of your rights, obligations, or benefits hereunder, by operation or law or otherwise, without our prior written consent.

(g) **No Third Party Beneficiaries**. The representations, warranties and other terms contained herein are for the sole benefit of the parties hereto and their respective successors and permitted assigns, and they shall not be construed as conferring any rights on any other persons.

(h) **Severability**. If any provision of these Auction Terms and Conditions is held by a court or arbitrator of competent jurisdiction to be contrary to law, such provision shall be changed by the court or by the arbitrator and interpreted so as to best accomplish the objectives of the original provision to the fullest extent allowed by law, and the remaining provisions of these Auction Terms and Conditions shall remain in full force and effect.

(i) **Notices**. Any notice or communication required or permitted to be given hereunder may be delivered by hand, deposited with an overnight courier, sent by email or mailed by registered or certified mail, return receipt requested, postage prepaid to the address for the other party first written above or at such other address as may hereafter be furnished in writing by either party hereto to the other party. Such notice will be deemed to have been given as of the date it is delivered, if by personal delivery or email; the next business day, if deposited with an overnight courier; and five days after being so mailed.

(j) **Headings**. The headings of the sections of these Auction Terms and Conditions are for convenience only and do not form a part hereof, and in no way limit, define, describe, modify, interpret or construe its meaning, scope or intent.

(k) **No Waiver**. No failure or delay on the part of either party in exercising any right, power or remedy under these Auction Terms and Conditions shall operate as a waiver, nor shall any single or partial exercise of any such right, power or remedy preclude any other or further exercise or the exercise of any other right, power or remedy.

(l) **Survival**. Sections of the Auction Terms and Conditions intended by their nature and content to survive termination of the Auction Terms and Conditions shall so survive.

I HAVE READ AND UNDERSTAND THESE AUCTION TERMS AND CONDITIONS AND AGREE TO COMPLY WITH THEM.

BIDDER

By: _____

(signature)

Name: _____

(please print)

Date: _____

ACKNOWLEDGED BY JULIEN'S AUCTIONS

By: _____

(signature)

Name: _____

(please print)

Title: _____

Date: _____